A *letter* FROM THE EDITOR...

EASY QUILTS

From eclectic to elegant, there is a quilt to satisfy every taste in *Easy Quilt Projects*. There are projects for every occasion, season, and style. What's more, with these simply creative projects, you'll have time to quilt up more gifts than ever before! Whether you're new to the art or an accomplished quiltmaker, you'll appreciate these inventive ideas to feed your creativity, simple solutions to sticky situations— and new challenges to test and hone your skills.

This book includes projects of every technique, sized for every space. It embraces a wide range of style. So you can expand your boundaries—tap into a new technique, select a style unlike any you've done before, dive into a different color palette, or jump into a different era. Because it's all covered here.

Quilting Basics is a comprehensive review that is as informative for accomplished quiltmakers as it is for beginners. Full-size patterns, understandable instructions, and step-by-step photos assure success, even if this is your first quilt project.

Slash and stack or fussy cut and hand quilt, this book will introduce interesting angles that open new doors to quilting delight.

HAPPY QUILTING!

features & CONTENTS

CHAPTER THREE: *Don't Stop Learning*

QUILTING BASICS:

gifts of the HEART

THE *gifting* OF A QUILT—FROM SELECTING FABRICS, TO PIECING, QUILTING, AND SIGNING—IS ONE OF LIFE'S GREATEST JOYS. HERE'S A COLLECTION OF PROJECTS FOR EVERY SPECIAL OCCASION; QUILTS THAT WILL EARN HEIRLOOM STATUS IMMEDIATELY.

petal
PERFECT

Strut YOUR STUFF WITH A PROJECT THAT LOOKS FAR MORE COMPLEX THAN IT IS. EASY APPLIQUÉ, SIMPLE TRIANGLE SQUARES—AND SMALL ENOUGH TO FINISH ON TIME!

Materials

⅜ yard of tan print for appliqué foundation and triangle-squares

½ yard of green print for leaf and stem appliqués, triangle-squares, and binding

18×22" piece (fat quarter) of blue print for flower appliqué and corner squares

⅜ yard of red print for flower appliqué and border strips

26" square of backing fabric

26" square of quilt batting

Freezer paper

Finished quilt top: 22" square

Quantities specified for 44/45"-wide, 100% cotton fabrics. All measurements include a ¼" seam allowance. Sew with right sides together unless otherwise stated.

Design: Lynette Jensen
Photographs: Scott Little;
    Marcia Cameron

Cut the Fabrics

To make the best use of your fabrics, cut the pieces in the order that follows. The Flower Pattern is *opposite*. To use freezer paper for appliquéing, as was done in this project, complete the following steps.

1. Lay the freezer paper, shiny side down, over the pattern. Use a pencil to trace the pattern the number of times indicated, leaving a ¼" space between tracings. Cut out each piece on the traced lines.

2. Press the freezer-paper shapes onto the wrong sides of the fabrics as designated, leaving ½" between shapes. Let the fabrics cool. Cut out fabric shapes roughly ¼" beyond the freezer-paper edges. Finger-press the seam allowances around the edges of the freezer-paper shapes.

From tan print, cut:
- 2—2⅞×42" strips
- 1—6½" square for appliqué foundation

From green print, cut:
- 2—2⅞×42" strips
- 3—2½×42" binding strips
- 1—1⅜×5" bias strip for stem appliqué (For instructions on cutting a bias strip, see Cut Bias Strips in Quilting Basics, which begins on *page 91*.)
- 1 of Flower Pattern

From blue print, cut:
- 16—2½" squares
- 1 of Flower Pattern

From red print, cut:
- 4—2½×18½" outer border strips
- 4—2½×10½" inner border strips
- 2 of Flower Pattern

Appliqué the Quilt Center

1. Fold the green print 1⅜×5" bias strip in half lengthwise with the wrong side inside; press. Stitch ¼" from the raw edges to keep them aligned. Fold the strip in half again, hiding the raw edges behind the first folded edge to create the flower stem; press.

2. Referring to the photograph *opposite* for placement, position the prepared stem and other appliqué pieces on the tan print 6½" square foundation; baste in place.

3. Using small slip stitches and threads in colors that match the fabrics, appliqué the pieces in place, starting with the stem and working from the bottom pieces to the top. Leave a ½" opening in the leaf and flower shapes for removing the freezer paper. Use the end of your needle to gently loosen the freezer paper from the fabric and pull it out. Hand-stitch the openings closed.

Assemble the Triangle-Squares

1. Layer a tan print 2⅞×42" strip with a green print 2⅞×42" strip to make a layered strip set; press to temporarily hold the strips together. Repeat to make a second layered strip set. Cut the layered strips into twenty 2⅞" squares (see Diagram 1).

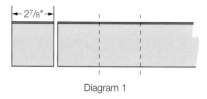

Diagram 1

2. Referring to Diagram 2 for placement, cut a pair of layered squares in half diagonally to make two sets of layered triangles. Stitch ¼" from the diagonal edges of each triangle pair. Press open to make two triangle-squares, pressing the seam allowances toward the green print triangles. Each pieced triangle-square should measure 2½" square, including the seam allowances.

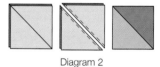

Diagram 2

3. Repeat Step 2 to make a total of 40 triangle-squares.

Assemble the Quilt Top

1. Referring to the photograph *opposite*, join three triangle-squares in a row to make a small triangle-square unit. Press the seam allowances in one direction. Repeat to make a total of four small triangle-square units.

2. Sew the small triangle-square units to opposite edges of the appliquéd foundation square. Press the seam allowances toward the appliquéd square. Add a blue print 2½" square to each end of the remaining small triangle-square units. Press the seam allowances toward the blue squares. Then join the units to the remaining edges of the appliquéd square to make the quilt center. Press the seam allowances toward the appliquéd square.

3. Sew the red print 2½×10½" inner border strips to opposite edges of the quilt center. Press the seam allowances toward the red border. Then join a blue print 2½" square to each end of the remaining red print inner border strips. Press the seam allowances toward the blue print squares. Add the units to the remaining edges of the quilt center.

4. Sew together seven triangle-squares in a row to make a large triangle-square unit. Press the seam allowances in one direction. Repeat to make a total of four large triangle-square units.

5. Sew the large triangle-square units to opposite edges of the quilt center. Press the seam allowances toward the quilt center. Add a blue print 2½" square to each end of the remaining large triangle-square units. Press the seam allowances toward the blue squares. Then join the units to the remaining edges of the quilt center. Press the seam allowances toward the quilt center.

6. Sew the red print 2½×18½" outer border strips to opposite edges of the quilt center. Press the seam allowances toward the red border. Then join a blue print 2½" square to each end of the remaining red print outer border strips.

Press the seam allowances toward the blue print squares. Add the units to the remaining edges of the quilt center to complete the quilt top.

Complete the Quilt

1. Layer the quilt top, batting, and backing according to the instructions in Quilting Basics, which begins on *page 91*. Quilt as desired.

2. Use the green print 2½×42" strips to bind the quilt according to the instructions in Quilting Basics.

Petal Perfect
Flower Pattern

primarily PRINTS

Materials

⅞ yard of solid white for borders

2 yards total of assorted red, yellow, and blue prints for blocks, pieced border, and binding

2¾ yards of yellow plaid flannel for backing

50" square of quilt batting

Finished quilt top: 43½" square
Finished block: 4" square

Quantities specified for 44/45"-wide, 100% cotton fabrics. All measurements include a ¼" seam allowance. Sew with right sides together unless otherwise stated.

Photographs: Perry Struse;
   Marcia Cameron

Cut the Fabrics

To make the best use of your fabrics, cut the pieces in the order that follows.

From solid white, cut:
- 2—3½×44" outer border strips
- 2—3½×38" outer border strips
- 2—1¾×35" inner border strips
- 2—1¾×32½" inner border strips
- 48—2" squares

From assorted prints, cut:
- 8—2×42" strips
- 16—1¾×42" strips
- 48—2" squares

Assemble the Blocks

1. Referring to the Strip Set Diagram for placement, sew together two assorted print 1¾×42" strips and one assorted print 2×42" strip to make a strip set. Press the seam allowances in one direction. Repeat to make a total of eight strip sets.

2. Cut each strip set into 4½"-wide segments. You'll need a total of 64 segments.

Assemble the Quilt Center

1. Referring to the photograph *opposite* and on *page 10* for placement, lay out the 64 segments in eight horizontal rows. Sew together the segments in each row. Press the seam allowances in one direction, alternating the direction with each row.

2. Join the rows to make the quilt center. Press the seam allowances in one direction. The pieced quilt center should measure 32½" square, including the seam allowances.

Strip Set Diagram

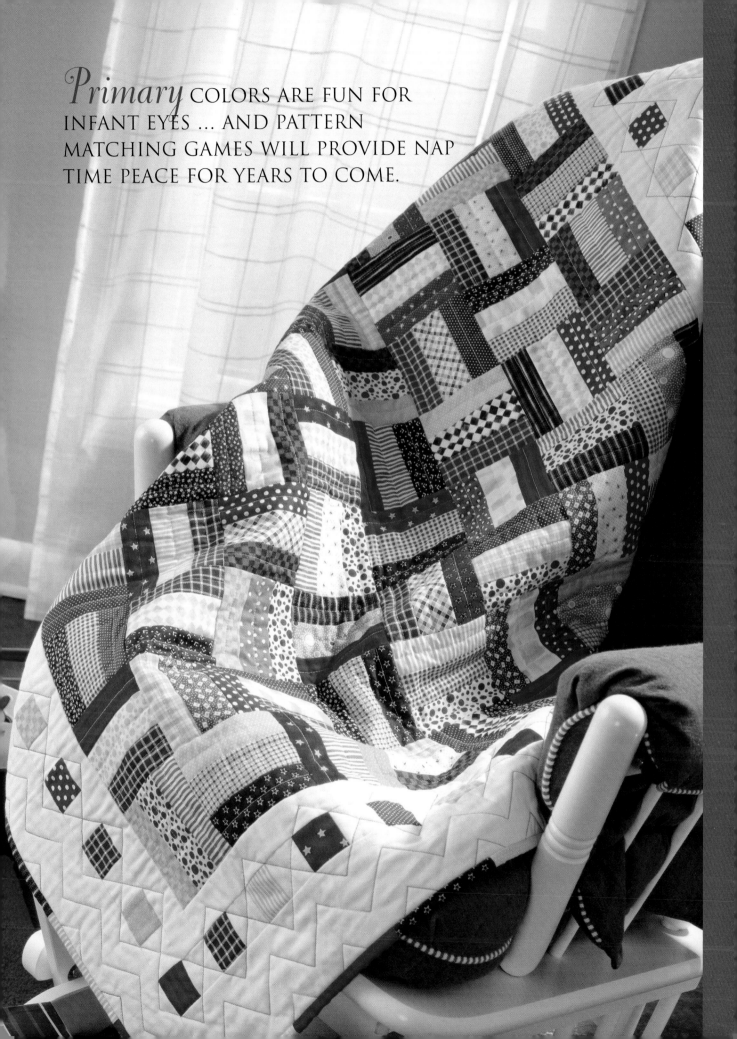

Primary COLORS ARE FUN FOR INFANT EYES … AND PATTERN MATCHING GAMES WILL PROVIDE NAP TIME PEACE FOR YEARS TO COME.

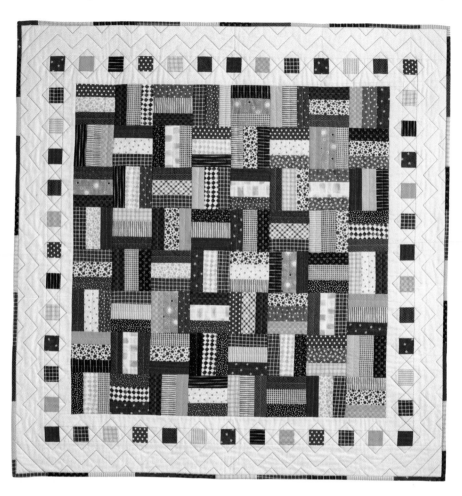

3. Sew together 12 solid white 2" squares and 13 assorted print 2" squares to make a pieced long border strip. The pieced long border strip should measure 2×38", including the seam allowances. Repeat to make a second pieced long border strip. Join the pieced border strips to the remaining edges of the pieced quilt center. Press the seam allowances toward the pieced border.

4. Sew the solid white 3½×38" outer border strips to opposite edges of the pieced quilt center. Then join the solid white 3½×44" outer border strips to the remaining edges of the pieced quilt center to complete the quilt top. Press the seam allowances toward the border.

Complete the Quilt
From assorted prints, cut and piece:
• Enough 2½"-wide pieces of varying length from 4½" to 6½" to total 180" in length

1. Layer the quilt top, batting, and backing according to the instructions in Quilting Basics, which begins on *page 91*. Quilt as desired.

2. Use the assorted print 2½"-wide pieced strip to bind the quilt according to the instructions in Quilting Basics.

Assemble and Add the Borders
1. Sew the solid white 1¾×32½" inner border strips to opposite edges of the pieced quilt center. Then join the solid white 1¾×35" inner border strips to the remaining edges of the pieced quilt center. Press the seam allowances toward the border.

2. Sew together 12 solid white 2" squares and 11 assorted print 2" squares to make a pieced short border strip. The pieced short border strip should measure 2×35", including the seam allowances. Repeat to make a second pieced short border strip. Sew the pieced border strips to opposite edges of the pieced quilt center.

THIS *quilt* WILL GROW WITH BABY!

Geese GALORE

TAKE A GANDER AT THIS *flock of geese*: THE MOSAIC THAT THEY FORM IS ENHANCED BY THE SIMPLE STRIP BORDER THAT ENCLOSES IT.

Materials

1 yard of white print for blocks
6—18×22" pieces (fat quarters) of assorted green prints for blocks and outer border
⅝ yard of pink print for blocks, inner border, and binding
2⅔ yards of backing fabric
47" square of quilt batting

Finished quilt top: 41" square
Finished block: 10" square

Quantities specified for 44/45"-wide, 100% cotton fabrics. All measurements include a ¼" seam allowance. Sew with right sides together unless otherwise stated.

Design: Darlene Zimmerman
Photographs: Perry Struse; Steve Struse

Cut the Fabrics

To make the best use of your fabrics, cut the pieces in the order that follows.

From white print, cut:
- 108—2⅞" squares, cutting each in half diagonally for a total of 216 triangles
- 12—1½×10½" sashing strips

From each green print, cut:
- 5—5¼" squares, cutting each diagonally twice in an X for a total of 20 triangles (you'll use 108 triangles out of the total of 120 cut)
- 17—2×4½" rectangles for outer border (you'll use 100 strips out of the total of 102 cut)

From pink print, cut:
- 5—2½×42" binding strips
- 4—1×42" strips for inner border
- 9—2½" squares
- 4—1½" squares

Assemble the Flying Geese Units

1. Referring to Diagram 1 for placement, sew together a white print triangle and a green print triangle. Press the seam allowance toward the green print triangle.

Diagram 1

2. Join a second white print triangle to the green print triangle to make a Flying Geese unit. Press the seam allowance toward the white print triangle. The pieced Flying Geese unit should measure 2½×4½", including the seam allowances.

3. Repeat to make a total of 108 Flying Geese units.

Assemble the Blocks

1. Referring to Diagram 2 for placement, lay out 12 Flying Geese units and one pink print 2½" square in sections in three horizontal rows.

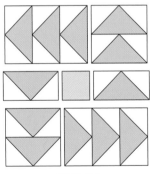

Diagram 2

2. Sew together the pieces in each row. Press the seam allowances toward the base of the Flying Geese units in the top and bottom rows and toward the center square in the middle row.

3. Join the rows to make a block. Press the seam allowances toward the middle

row. The pieced block should measure 10½" square, including the seam allowances.

4. Repeat steps 1 through 3 to make a total of nine blocks.

Assemble the Quilt Center

1. Referring to the Quilt Assembly Diagram and the photograph *opposite* for placement, lay out the nine pieced blocks, the white print 1½×10½" sashing strips, and the pink print 1½" squares in five horizontal rows.

Quilt Assembly Diagram

2. Sew together the pieces in each row. Press the seam allowances toward the white print sashing strips. Then join the rows to complete the quilt center. Press the seam allowances toward the sashing strips. The pieced quilt center should measure 32½" square, including the seam allowances.

Assemble and Add the Borders

1. Cut and piece the pink print 1×42" strips into the following:
- 2—1×33½" inner border strips
- 2—1×32½" inner border strips

2. Sew the short pink print inner border strips to opposite edges of the pieced quilt center. Press the seam allowances toward the pink print border. Add the long pink print inner border strips to the remaining edges of the pieced quilt center. Press the seam allowances toward the pink print border.

3. Aligning long edges, join 22 assorted green print 2×4½" rectangles to make a short border unit that measures 4½×33½", including the seam allowances. Press the seam allowances in one direction. Repeat to make a second short border unit.

4. Center and sew the short border units to opposite edges of the quilt center. Press the seam allowances toward the pieced outer border. Trim any excess border fabric from each end.

5. Aligning long edges, sew together 28 assorted green print 2×4½" rectangles to make a long border unit. Press the seam allowances in one direction. Repeat to make a second long border unit.

6. Center and sew the long border units to the remaining edges of the pieced quilt center. Trim the excess border fabric from each end to complete the quilt top.

Complete the Quilt

1. Layer the quilt top, batting, and backing according to the instructions in Quilting Basics, which begins on *page 91*. Quilt as desired.

2. Use the pink print 2½×42" strips to bind the quilt according to the instructions in Quilting Basics.

flower FARM

FUSSY-CUT *flowers* ARE FRAMED IN GARDEN
PATHS CREATED BY SIMPLE GEOMETRIC SHAPES.

Materials

$1\frac{3}{4}$ yards of floral bouquet print for
  blocks (choose a bouquet design that
  has dense floral areas, as well as areas
  with tendrils, leaves, and buds)
$\frac{7}{8}$ yard of dark green print for blocks
$\frac{3}{4}$ yard of light green print for block and
  inner border squares
$3\frac{1}{2}$ yards of rose print for blocks, outer
  border, binding, and backing
$\frac{7}{8}$ yard of off-white small print for setting
  triangles and inner border
52×69" of quilt batting

Finished quilt top: $46\frac{1}{4}$×63"
Finished blocks: $6\frac{1}{2}$" square

Quantities specified for 44/45"-wide,
100% cotton fabrics. All measurements
include a $\frac{1}{4}$" seam allowance. Sew
with right sides together unless
otherwise stated.

Design: Sharon Yenter
Photograph: Perry Struse

Cut the Fabrics

To make the best use of your fabrics, cut
the pieces in the order that follows. The
border strips are cut the length of the
fabric (parallel to the selvage). The
pattern is on *page 16*. To make a template
of the pattern, follow the instructions in
Quilting Basics, which begins on *page 91*.

From floral bouquet print, cut:
- 8—$6\frac{1}{2}$" squares from dense floral area
- 8—3×$6\frac{1}{2}$" rectangles from dense
  floral area
- 16—3×$6\frac{1}{2}$" rectangles from tendril,
  leaf, and bud areas
- 8—$2\frac{5}{8}$" squares from dense floral area,
  cutting each diagonally in half for a
  total of 16 Block 3 triangles
- 16—$2\frac{5}{8}$" squares from tendril, leaf,
  and bud areas, cutting each diagonally
  in half for a total of 32 Block 3
  triangles

From dark green print, cut:
- 24—$2\frac{1}{4}$×$6\frac{1}{2}$" rectangles
- 34 of Flower Pattern

From light green print, cut:
- 24—$2\frac{1}{4}$×$6\frac{1}{2}$" rectangles
- 10—3" squares for inner border
- 24 of Flower Pattern

From rose print, cut:
- 2—3×$63\frac{1}{2}$" outer border strips
- 2—3×$41\frac{3}{4}$" outer border strips
- 5—2×42" binding strips
- 17—3" squares

From off-white small print, cut:
- 2—12" squares, cutting each
  diagonally twice in an X for a total of
  8 setting triangles (you'll have 2
  leftover triangles)
- 2—$7\frac{5}{8}$" squares, cutting each in half
  diagonally for a total of 4 corner
  triangles
- 6—3×$14\frac{3}{4}$" strips for inner border
- 4—3×$11\frac{1}{2}$" strips for inner border
- 4—3×9" strips for inner border

Assemble the Blocks

Block 1
Referring to Diagram 1 for placement,
sew together one light green print
$2\frac{1}{4}$×$6\frac{1}{2}$" rectangle, one dark green print
$2\frac{1}{4}$×$6\frac{1}{2}$" rectangle, and one floral
bouquet print 3×$6\frac{1}{2}$" rectangle from
dense floral area to make a Block 1. Press
the seam allowances toward the green
print rectangles. Repeat to make a total
of eight of Block 1.

Block 2
Join a light green print $2\frac{1}{4}$×$6\frac{1}{2}$"
rectangle, a dark green print $2\frac{1}{4}$×$6\frac{1}{2}$"

Diagram 1

Diagram 2

rectangle, and a floral bouquet 3×6½" rectangle from tendril, leaf, or bud area to make a Block 2 (see Diagram 2 on *page 14*); press. Repeat to make a total of 16 of Block 2.

Block 3

Sew together one rose print 3" square, two light green flower pattern pieces, two dark green flower pattern pieces, two dense floral Block 3 triangles, and two tendril, leaf, or bud Block 3 triangles in three diagonal rows (see Diagram 3). Press the seam allowances in each row in one direction, alternating the direction with each row. Then join the rows to make a Block 3. Press seam allowances in one direction. Repeat to make a total of six of Block 3.

Diagram 3   Diagram 4

Block 4

Referring to Diagram 4 for placement, sew together one rose print 3" square, two light green flower pattern pieces, two dark green flower pattern pieces, and four dense floral Block 3 triangles in three diagonal rows. Press the seam allowances in each row in one direction, alternating the direction with each row. Then join the rows to make a Block 4. Press the seam allowances in one direction.

Block 5

Referring to Diagram 5 for placement, sew together one rose print 3" square, one light green flower pattern piece, two dark green flower pattern pieces, and two tendril, leaf, or bud Block 3 triangles in diagonal rows. Press the seam allowances

Diagram 5

in each row in one direction, alternating the direction with each row. Then join the rows to make a Block 5. Press the seam allowances in one direction. Repeat to make a total of 10 of Block 5.

Assemble the Quilt Center

1. Referring to the Quilt Assembly Diagram for placement, lay out the blocks and six off-white small print setting triangles in diagonal rows.

Quilt Assembly Diagram

2. Sew together the blocks in each diagonal row. Combine pairs of diagonal rows when necessary to add the setting triangles. Add the setting triangles, then join the diagonal rows. Add the off-white small print corner triangles to each corner to complete the quilt center.

Add the Borders

1. Sew one light green print 3" square to each end of an off-white small print 3×14¾" strip. Then join one off-white small print 3×9" strip to each end of the strip to make a pieced border strip. Press all seam allowances toward the green squares. Repeat to make a second pieced border strip.

2. Sew the pieced border strips to the top and bottom edges of the quilt center; press.

3. Beginning with a light green print 3" square, join three light green print 3" squares with two off-white small print 3×14¾" strips, alternating pieces. Then join an off-white small print 3×11½" strip to each end to make a pieced border strip. Press all seam allowances toward the green squares. Sew the pieced border strips to the side edges of the quilt center; press.

4. Sew the rose print 3×41¾" outer border strips to the top and bottom edges of the quilt center; press.

5. Sew the rose print 3×63½" outer border strips to the side edges of the quilt center to complete the quilt top; press.

Complete the Quilt

1. Layer the quilt top, batting, and backing according to the instructions in Quilting Basics, which begins on *page 91*. Quilt as desired.

2. Use the rose print 2×42" strips to bind the quilt according to the instructions in Quilting Basics.

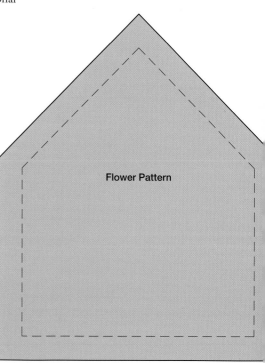

Flower Pattern

BEAR *Tracks*

O START *piecing*, PICK A PROJECT WITH SQUARES AND TRIANGLES, LIKE THIS LAP-SIZE QUILT. THEN HEAD TO THE CUTTING AND SEWING TABLE AND PRACTICE YOUR MACHINE PIECING SKILLS.

Materials

4—⅓-yard pieces of assorted cream and
    tan prints for blocks
8—¼-yard pieces of assorted green, red,
    blue, brown, black, and gold prints
    for blocks
1¼ yards of black print for border and
    binding
2¾ yards of backing fabric
49×61" of quilt batting

Finished quilt top: 44×56"
Finished block: 12" square

Quantities specified for 44/45"-wide,
100% cotton fabrics. All measurements
include a ¼" seam allowance. Sew
with right sides together unless
otherwise stated.

Design: Darlene Zimmerman
Photographs: Perry Struse;
    Marcia Cameron

Cut the Fabrics

To make the best use of your fabrics, cut
the pieces in the order that follows.

*From each assorted cream and tan print,
cut:*
• 24—2⅞" squares, cutting each in half
    diagonally for a total of 48 triangles
• 12—2½" squares
*From each assorted green, red, blue, brown,
black, and gold print, cut:*
• 6—4½" squares
• 12—2⅞" squares, cutting each in half
    diagonally for a total of 24 triangles

Assemble the Bear's Paw Blocks

In this project, each unit in a Bear's Paw
block requires just two prints, one for the
background (cream or tan) and one for
the bear's paw (green, red, blue, brown,
black, or gold). For ease in assembly,
group the cream and tan print pieces into
sets of four triangles and one 2½" square
of the same color for the background.
Then group the green, red, blue, brown,
black, and gold print pieces into sets of
four triangles and one 4½" square of the
same color for the bear's paw.

1. Select one set of background pieces
and one set of bear's paw pieces.

2. Join one background triangle and one
bear's paw triangle to make a triangle-
square (see Diagram 1). Press the seam
allowance toward the darker fabric. The
pieced triangle-square should measure
2½" square. Repeat to make a total of
four matching triangle-squares.

Diagram 1

3. Referring to Diagram 2, lay out the
four triangle-squares, the background
2½" square, and the bear's paw 4½"
square. Sew together the pieces in
sections. Then join the sections to make a
Bear's Paw unit. The pieced unit should
measure 6½" square, including the seam
allowances.

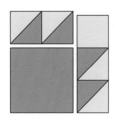

Diagram 2

4. Repeat steps 1 through 3 to make a
total of 48 Bear's Paw units.

5. Referring to Diagram 3 for placement,
sew together four Bear's Paw units of
different colors in pairs. Press the seam

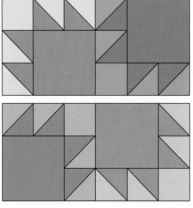

Diagram 3

allowances in opposite directions. Then
join the pairs to make a Bear's Paw block.
Press the seam allowance in one
direction. The pieced Bear's Paw block
should measure 12½" square, including
the seam allowances.

6. Repeat Step 5 to make a total of 12
Bear's Paw blocks.

Assemble the Quilt Center

1. Referring to the photograph *opposite*
for placement, lay out the 12 pieced
blocks in four horizontal rows. Sew
together the blocks in each row. Press the
seam allowances in one direction,
alternating the direction with each row.

2. Join the four rows to make the quilt
center. The pieced quilt center should
measure 36½×48½", including the seam
allowances.

Add the Border

From black print, cut:
• 5—4½×42" strips for border
• 6—2½×42" binding strips

1. Cut and piece the black print 4½×42"
strips to make the following:
• 2—4½×48½" border strips
• 2—4½×44½" border strips

2. Sew the long black print border strips
to the side edges of the pieced quilt
center. Then join the short black print
border strips to the top and bottom
edges of the pieced quilt center to
complete the quilt top. Press all seam
allowances toward the black print border.

Complete the Quilt

1. Layer the quilt top, batting, and
backing according to the instructions in
Quilting Basics, which begins on *page 91.*
Quilt as desired.

2. Use the black print 2½×42" strips to
bind the quilt according to the
instructions in Quilting Basics.

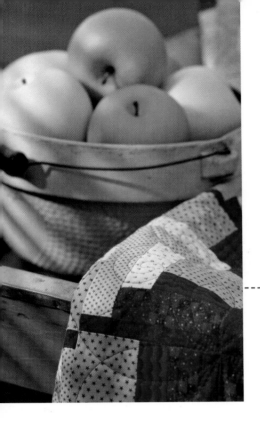

Autumn LIGHTS

IN THE *warm colors* OF FALL, THESE LOG CABIN BLOCKS BECOME A CELEBRATION OF SUMMER'S END; A WAVING QUILT MOTIF WELCOMES AUTUMN.

Materials

1¾ yards of gold print for blocks, middle border, and binding
½ yard of red print No. 1 for blocks
¾ yard of red print No. 2 for blocks
⅝ yard of light beige print for blocks
¾ yard of beige print for blocks
⅞ yard of dark red print No. 1 for blocks
1¼ yards of dark red print No. 2 for inner and outer borders
3½ yards of backing fabric
64×82" of quilt batting

Finished quilt top: 57½×75½"
Finished block: 9" square

Quantities specified for 44/45"-wide, 100% cotton fabrics. All measurements include a ¼" seam allowance. Sew with right sides together unless otherwise stated.

Design: Fiber Mosaics
Photographs: Perry Struse; Steve Struse

Cut the Fabrics

To make the best use of your fabrics, cut the pieces in the order that follows.

From gold print, cut:
- 7—2½×42" binding strips

- 6—2×42" strips for middle border
- 140—2½×3" rectangles
From red print No. 1, cut:
- 140—1½×3" rectangles
From red print No. 2, cut:
- 140—1½×4" rectangles
From light beige print, cut:
- 140—1½×3½" rectangles
From beige print, cut:
- 140—1½×4½" rectangles
From dark red print No.1, cut:
- 140—1×5" rectangles
From dark red print No. 2, cut:
- 7—4½×42" strips for outer border
- 6—1¼×42" strips for inner border

Assemble the Blocks

1. Sew a red print No. 1—1½×3" rectangle to a long edge of a gold print 2½×3" rectangle (see Diagram 1). Press seam allowance toward gold rectangle.

Diagram 1   Diagram 2

2. Sew a light beige print 1½×3½" rectangle to the right edge of the pieced unit (see Diagram 2). Press the seam allowance toward the gold print rectangle.

3. Sew a red print No. 2—1½×4" rectangle to the bottom edge of the pieced unit (see Diagram 3). Press seam allowance toward gold print rectangle.

Diagram 3   Diagram 4

4. Sew a beige print 1½×4½" rectangle to the right edge of the pieced unit (see Diagram 4). Press the seam allowance toward the gold print rectangle.

5. Sew a dark red print No. 1—1×5" rectangle to the bottom edge of the pieced unit to complete a quarter block (see Diagram 5). Press seam allowance toward gold print rectangle.

Diagram 5

6. Repeat steps 1 through 5 to make a total of 140 quarter units.

7. Sew together four quarter units in pairs (see Diagram 6). Press the seam allowances in opposite directions. Then join the pairs to make a block. Press the seam allowances in one direction. The pieced block should measure $9^{1}/2$" square, including the seam allowances. Repeat to make a total of 35 pieced blocks.

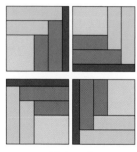

Diagram 6

Assemble the Quilt Center

1. Referring to the photograph *right* for placement, lay out the pieced blocks in seven horizontal rows.

2. Sew together the blocks in each horizontal row. Press the seam allowances in one direction, alternating the direction with each row. Then join the rows to complete the quilt center. The pieced quilt center should measure $45^{1}/2 \times 63^{1}/2$", including the seam allowances.

Add the Borders

1. Cut and piece the dark red print No. 2 $1^{1}/4 \times 42$" strips to make the following:
• 2—$1^{1}/4 \times 65$" inner border strips
• 2—$1^{1}/4 \times 45^{1}/2$" inner border strips

2. Sew the short inner border strips to the top and bottom edges of the pieced quilt center. Then add the long inner border strips to the side edges of the pieced quilt center. Press the seam allowances toward the red print border.

3. Cut and piece the gold print 2×42" strips to make the following:
• 2—2×68" middle border strips
• 2—2×47" middle border strips

4. Sew the short middle border strips to the top and bottom edges of the pieced quilt center. Then add the long middle border strips to the side edges of the pieced quilt center. Press the seam allowances toward the gold print border.

5. Cut and piece the dark red print No. 2 $4^{1}/2 \times 42$" strips to make the following:
• 2—$4^{1}/2 \times 76$" outer border strips
• 2—$4^{1}/2 \times 50$" outer border strips

6. Sew the short outer border strips to the top and bottom edges of the pieced quilt center. Then add the long outer border strips to the side edges of the pieced quilt center to complete the quilt top. Press the seam allowances toward the red print border.

Complete the Quilt

1. Layer the quilt top, batting, and backing according to the instructions in Quilting Basics, which begins on *page 91*. Quilt as desired.

2. Use the gold print $2^{1}/2 \times 42$" strips to bind the quilt according to the instructions in Quilting Basics.

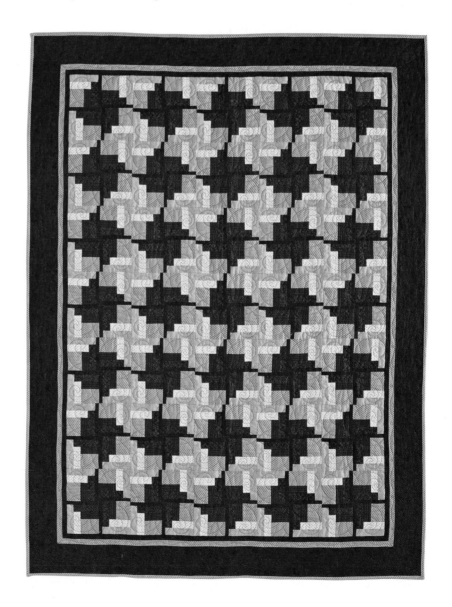

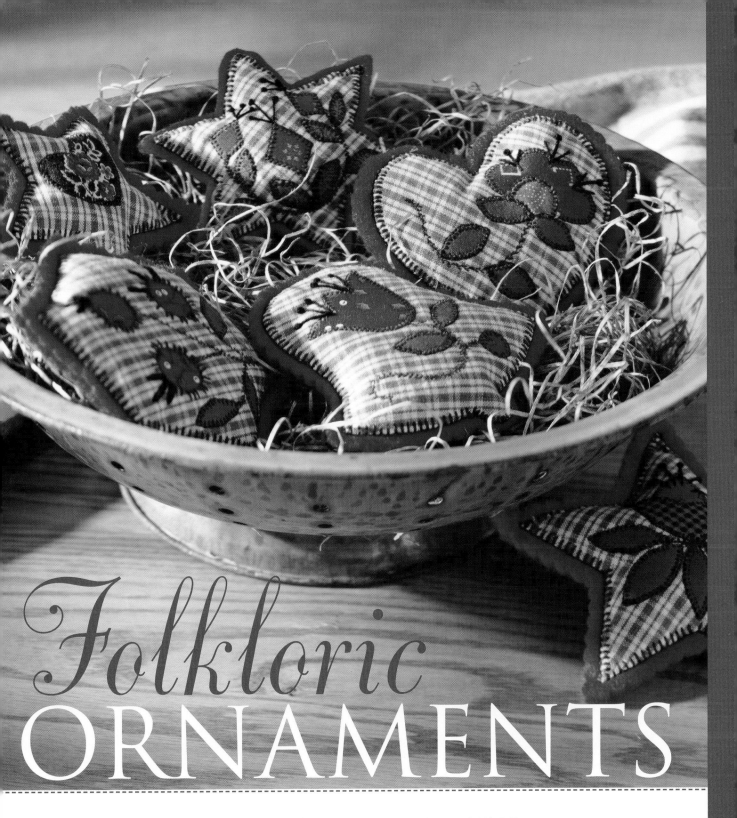

Folkloric ORNAMENTS

SHARE YOUR PASSION FOR QUILTING
WITH FRIENDS AND FAMILY BY MAKING THESE
QUICK-AND-EASY *ornaments.*

Materials for One Ornament

2—7" squares of red heavyweight
   wool-like felt for ornament front
   and back
1—6" square of blue plaid for
   background appliqué
Scraps of assorted solid green, red, and
   orange-and-black plaid prints for
   appliqués
¼ yard of fusible web
Black embroidery floss
Scalloped-edge pinking scissors
Scraps of fiberfill stuffing

Design: Nancy Brenan Daniel
Photograph: Perry Struse

The following instructions are for
Ornament A. The patterns are on *pages
25 and 26.* Follow these same steps to
make ornaments B through F.

Cut and Prepare the Appliqué Pieces

1. Lay the fusible web, paper side up,
over the patterns. Use a pencil to trace
each pattern the number of times
indicated. Cut out the pieces roughly ¼"
outside the traced lines.

2. Following the manufacturer's
instructions, press the fusible-web shapes
onto the back of the designated fabrics.
Let the fabric cool. Cut out the shapes
on the drawn lines. Peel off paper
backings.

From blue plaid, cut:
• 1 of Pattern A
From solid green scraps, cut:
• 2 of Pattern B
• 3 of Pattern C
From red print scrap, cut:
• 1 of Pattern D
From orange-and-black plaid scrap, cut:
• 1 of Pattern E

Assemble Ornament A

1. Press the blue plaid star onto a red felt
7" square. Referring to the Assembly
Diagram, position the prepared flower
and leaf appliqué pieces on the blue plaid
star unit. Fuse in place.

Assembly Diagram
Ornament A

2. Thread your sewing machine with two
strands of black thread. With a small-size
blanket stitch, stitch the flower and leaf
shapes in place. Then blanket-stitch the
blue plaid star to one of the red felt
squares.

3. With two strands of black embroidery
floss, straight-stitch the flower details on
the ornament by hand; add a French knot
at the end of the straight stitching.

   To make a French knot, refer to the
diagram *above right.* Pull the thread
through at the point where the knot is
desired (A). Wrap the thread around the
needle twice without twisting it. Insert
the tip of the needle into the fabric at B,
1/16" away from A. Gently push the wraps
down the needle to meet the fabric. Pull
the needle and trailing thread through
the fabric slowly and smoothly.

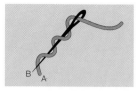

French Knot

4. With wrong sides together, layer the
appliquéd star unit and the remaining red
felt 7" square. Stitch the two layers
together along the edge of the blue plaid
star, leaving a small opening for stuffing.

5. With scalloped-edge pinking scissors,
cut the red felt ¼" from the edge of the
blue plaid star. Stuff the ornament lightly.
Machine-stitch the opening closed.

6. With three strands of black
embroidery floss, make a 2½" hanging
loop to complete the ornament.

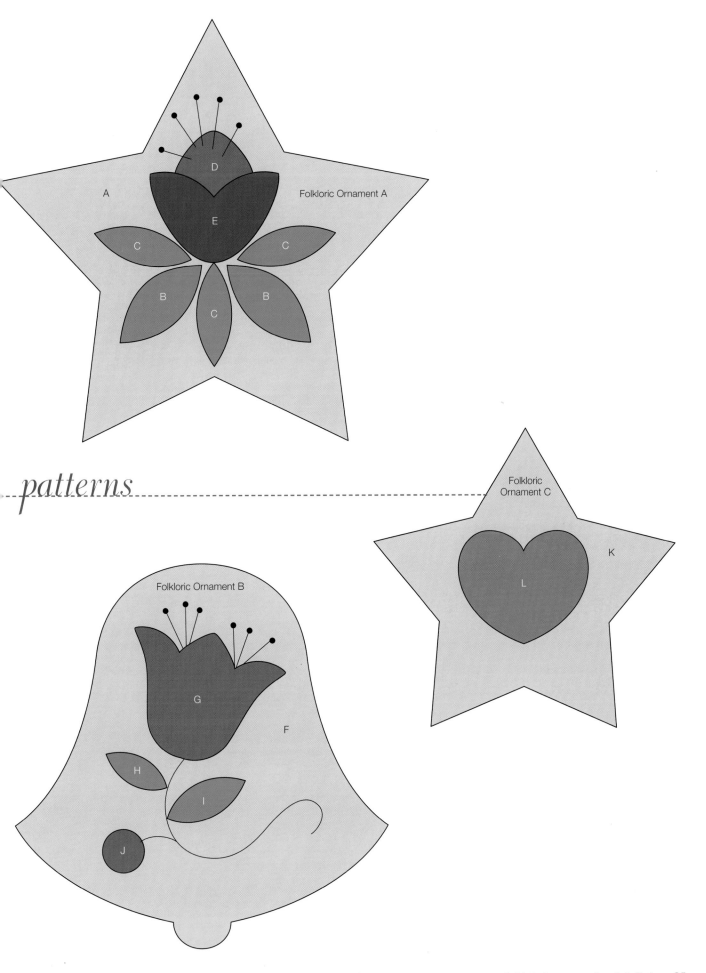

Folkloric Ornament A

Folkloric Ornament C

patterns

Folkloric Ornament B

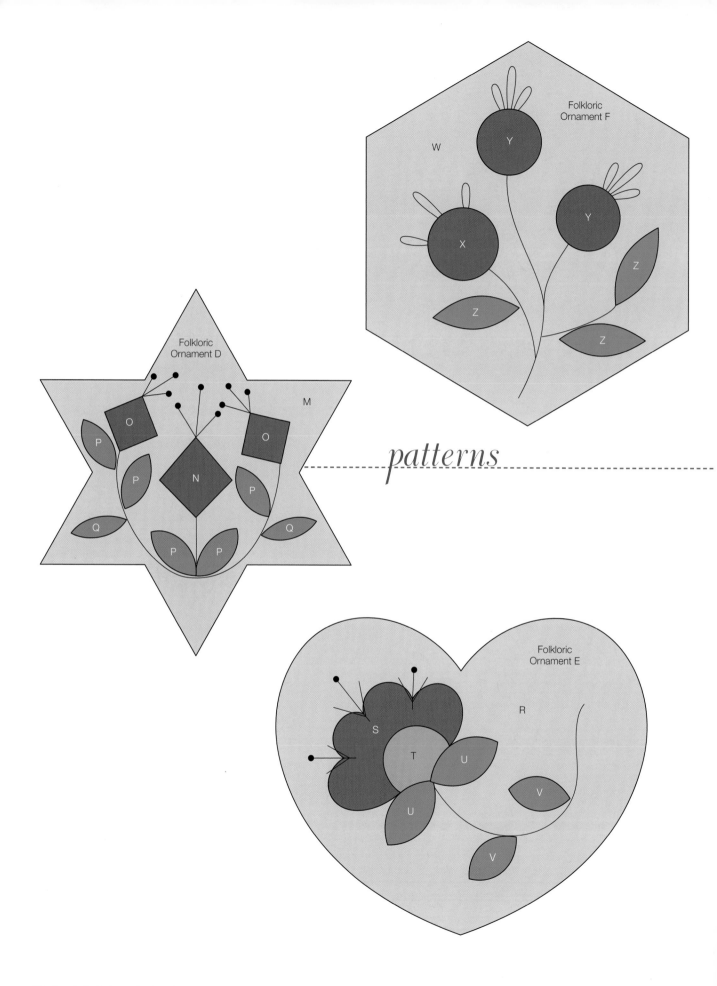

Folkloric
Ornament F

W

Y

X

Y

Z

Z

Z

Folkloric
Ornament D

M

O

O

P

P

N

P

Q

P

P

Q

patterns

Folkloric
Ornament E

R

S

T

U

U

V

V

TREASURED *Memories*

A *combination* OF TWO TRADITIONAL BLOCKS—NINE-PATCH AND HOUR GLASS—REPRESENTS THE MIRACULOUS MERGING THAT TRANSFORMS LOVING PEOPLE INTO FAMILY.

Materials

2¼ yards of burgundy print for blocks, border, and binding

2 yards of beige print for blocks and border

¼ yard *each* of blue, orange, yellow, and green prints for blocks

3¾ yards of backing fabric

64×82" of quilt batting

Finished quilt top: 57¾×75¾"
Finished block: 9" square

Quantities specified for 44/45"-wide, 100% cotton fabrics. All measurements include a ¼" seam allowance. Sew with right sides together unless otherwise stated.

Design: Elizabeth Bailey
Photograph: Steve Struse

Cut the Fabrics

To make the best use of your fabrics, cut the pieces in the order that follows.

From burgundy print, cut:
- 7—2¾×42" binding strips
- 15—10¼" squares, cutting each diagonally twice in an X for a total of 60 triangles (you'll have two leftover triangles)
- 18—3½" squares

From beige print, cut:
- 16—10¼" squares, cutting each diagonally twice in an X for a total of 64 triangles (you'll have two leftover triangles)
- 72—3½" squares

From blue print, cut:
- 20—3½" squares

From orange print, cut:
- 20—3½" squares

From yellow print, cut:
- 16—3½" squares

From green print, cut:
- 16—3½" squares

Assemble the Nine-Patch Blocks

1. Referring to Diagram 1 for placement, lay out four beige print 3½" squares, one burgundy print 3½" square, and four blue print 3½" squares in three horizontal rows.

Diagram 1

2. Sew together the squares in each row. Press the seam allowances toward the blue print squares. Then join the rows to make a blue Nine-Patch block. Press the seam allowances in one direction. The pieced blue Nine-Patch block should measure 9½" square, including the seam allowances.

3. Repeat steps 1 and 2 to make a total of five blue Nine-Patch blocks.

4. In the same manner, make a total of five orange Nine-Patch blocks, four yellow Nine-Patch blocks, and four green Nine-Patch blocks.

Assemble the Hour Glass Blocks

1. Referring to Diagram 2 for placement, sew together two burgundy print triangles and two beige print triangles in pairs. Press the seam allowances toward the burgundy print triangles. Then join the pairs to make an Hour Glass block. Press the seam allowances in one direction. The pieced Hour Glass block should measure 9½" square, including the seam allowances.

Diagram 2

2. Repeat Step 1 to make a total of 17 Hour Glass blocks.

Assemble the Quilt Center

1. Referring to the photograph at *right* for placement, lay out the Nine-Patch blocks and the Hour Glass blocks in seven horizontal rows, alternating the blocks. Sew together the blocks in each row. Press the seam allowances toward the Hour Glass blocks.

2. Join the rows to complete the quilt center. Press the seam allowances in one direction. The pieced quilt center should measure 45½×63½", including the seam allowances.

Assemble and Add the Border

1. Referring to Diagram 3 for placement, join seven burgundy print triangles and eight beige print triangles in a row to make a side border unit. Press the seam allowances toward the burgundy print triangles. Repeat to make a second side border unit.

2. Aligning each border unit's burgundy print triangles with the quilt center's edges, sew a side border unit to each side edge of the quilt center, stopping ¼" from each corner.

3. Referring to Diagram 4 for placement, sew together five burgundy print triangles and six beige print triangles to make a top border unit. Press the seam allowances toward the burgundy print triangles. Repeat to make a bottom border unit.

4. Aligning each border unit's burgundy print triangles with the quilt center's edges, sew the top and bottom border units to the top and bottom edges of the quilt center, stopping ¼" from each corner.

5. Finish each corner with a diagonal seam (see Diagram 5).

Complete the Quilt

1. Layer the quilt top, batting, and backing according to the instructions in Quilting Basics, which begins on *page 91*.

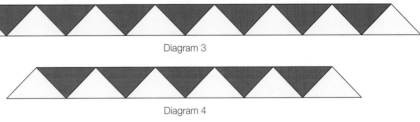

Diagram 3

Diagram 4

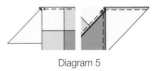

Diagram 5

2. Quilt as desired. Elizabeth hand-quilted Xs and hearts in the Nine-Patch blocks and used a stencil with a heart and leaves in each of the Hour Glass block triangles.

3. Use the burgundy 2¾×42" strips to bind the quilt according to the instructions in Quilting Basics.

Celebrate EACH Season

2

Quilts AREN'T QUARANTINED IN THE BEDROOM ANYMORE! TODAY, QUILTMAKERS WARM EVERY CORNER—AND ADD COLOR TO EVERY SETTING—WITH QUILTS OF COLOR AND STYLE. HERE'S A COLLECTION OF QUILTS THAT REFLECT THE DELIGHT OF EVERY SEASON.

DAISY *pillow*

USHER IN SPRING LONG BEFORE THE CONEFLOWERS BLOOM WITH THIS DAISY PILLOW. FUSE THE DAISIES, THEN MACHINE-STITCH AROUND THEM: *easy appliqué!*

Materials

¼ yard of yellow print for appliqué foundations

⅛ yard of green print for sashing and border

⅝ yard of yellow floral for borders and pillow back

⅛ yard of dark purple print for flower appliqués

1—6" square of light purple print for flower appliqués

1—6" square of gold print for flower appliqués

⅛ yard of solid green for flower appliqués

½ yard of lightweight fusible web

24" square of quilt batting

18" square pillow form

Finished pillow: 18" square

Quantities specified for 44/45"-wide, 100% cotton fabrics. All measurements include a ¼" seam allowance. Sew with right sides together unless otherwise stated.

Design: Teri Christopherson
Photograph: Perry Struse

Cut the Fabrics

To make the best use of your fabrics, cut the pieces in the order that follows. The patterns are *opposite*. To use fusible web for appliquéing, as was done in this project, complete the following steps.

1. Lay the fusible web, paper side up, over the patterns. Use a pencil to trace each pattern the number of times indicated, leaving a ½" space between tracings. Cut out each piece roughly ¼" outside the traced lines.

2. Following the manufacturer's instructions, press the fusible-web shapes onto the wrong sides of the designated fabrics; let cool. Cut out the fabric shapes on the drawn lines. Peel off the paper backing.

From yellow print, cut:
• 4—6½" squares for appliqué foundations

From green print, cut:
• 3—1×42" strips for sashing and middle border

From yellow floral, cut:
• 4—1½×42" strips for inner and outer borders
• 2—13×18½" rectangles for pillow back

From dark purple print, cut:
• 4 *each* of patterns A, B, and D

From light purple print, cut:
• 4 of Pattern C

From gold print, cut:
• 4 of Pattern E

From solid green, cut:
• 8 of Pattern G
• 4 of Pattern F

Appliqué and Assemble the Pillow Center

1. Referring to the Appliqué Placement Diagram, position the appliqué pieces on the four yellow print 6½" square appliqué foundations, overlapping as shown; fuse in place.

2. Using matching thread, machine-blanket-stitch around each fused piece to make four appliquéd blocks.

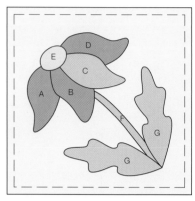

Appliqué Placement Diagram

3. Referring to the photograph on *page 39* for placement, lay out the appliquéd blocks in two horizontal rows. Sew together the squares in each row. Press the seam allowances in opposite directions. Then join the rows to make the pillow center. Press the seam allowance in one direction. The pieced pillow center should measure 12½" square, including the seam allowances.

Assemble the Pillow Top

1. Cut and piece the green print 1×42" strips to make the following:
• 2—1×16½" middle border strips
• 2—1×15½" middle border strips
• 2—1×13½" sashing strips
• 2—1×12½" sashing strips

2. Cut and piece the yellow floral 1½×42" strips to make the following:
• 2—1½×18½" outer border strips
• 2—1½×16½" outer border strips
• 2—1½×15½" inner border strips
• 2—1½×13½" inner border strips

3. Sew the short green print sashing strips to opposite edges of the pieced pillow center. Then add the long green print sashing strips to the remaining edges of the pillow center. Press the seam allowances toward the green print sashing.

4. Sew the short yellow floral inner border strips to opposite edges of the pieced pillow center. Then add the long yellow floral inner border strips to the remaining edges of the pieced pillow center. Press the seam allowances toward the yellow floral border.

5. Sew the short green print middle border strips to opposite edges of the pieced pillow center. Then add the long green print middle border strips to the remaining edges of the pillow center. Press the seam allowances toward the green print border.

6. Sew the short yellow floral outer border strips to opposite edges of the pieced pillow center. Then add the long

yellow floral outer border strips to the remaining edges of the pillow center to complete the pillow top. Press the seam allowances toward the yellow floral border. The pieced pillow top should measure 18½" square, including the seam allowances.

Quilt the Pillow Top
1. Layer the pieced pillow top and batting; baste together.

2. Quilt as desired. Designer Teri Christopherson machine-quilted an echo pattern around the daisy appliqués and in the ditch along the border seam lines.

Complete the Pillow
1. Turn a long edge of a yellow floral 13×18½" rectangle under 1"; press. Turn the same edge under another 1"; press. Topstitch the folded edge in place. Repeat with the remaining yellow floral 13×18½" rectangle.

2. Overlap the folded edges by about 4" (see Pillow Back Diagram); stitch the

pieces in place, sewing across the folded edges, to create a pillow back.

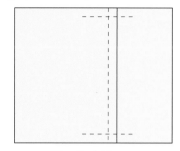

Pillow Back Diagram

3. Trim the pillow back to 18½" square.

4. Layer the pillow top and pillow back; join to make the pillow cover.

5. Trim the pillow back and corner the seam allowances, if needed, to reduce bulk. Turn the pillow cover right side out. Use a blunt object to carefully poke out the corners. Insert the pillow form through the back opening to complete the pillow.

patterns

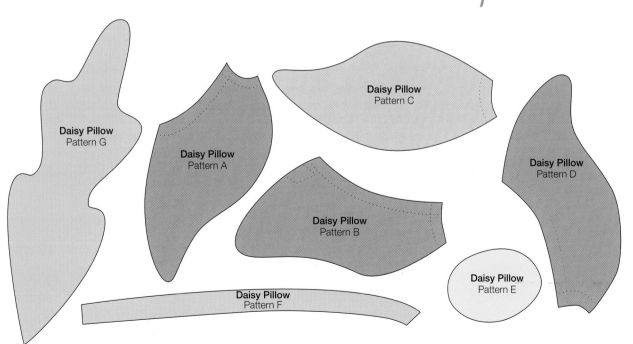

Daisy Pillow
Pattern G

Daisy Pillow
Pattern A

Daisy Pillow
Pattern C

Daisy Pillow
Pattern D

Daisy Pillow
Pattern B

Daisy Pillow
Pattern E

Daisy Pillow
Pattern F

Summer skies, GOLDEN SUN, A BOAT SAILING ON WAVES OF BLUE: THE FRESH OCEAN BREEZE IS ALMOST TANGIBLE, EVEN FAR FROM THE SEA.

fun in the SUN!

Materials

1 yard of light blue print for blocks
$\frac{1}{2}$ yard of white print for blocks
    and inner border
$\frac{5}{8}$ yard of red print for blocks and
    middle border
$\frac{1}{4}$ yard of blue print for sashing
$\frac{3}{4}$ yard of dark blue print No. 1 for
    sashing, outer border, and binding
$\frac{1}{8}$ yard of dark blue print No. 2 for
    sashing
$\frac{1}{8}$ yard of dark blue print No. 3 for
    sashing
$\frac{1}{8}$ yard of light gold print for blocks
$\frac{1}{8}$ yard of dark gold print for blocks
    and borders
2 yards of backing fabric
48×52" of quilt batting

Finished quilt top: 42×46"
Finished boat block: 8" square
Finished star block: 4" square

Quantities specified for 44/45"-wide,
100% cotton fabrics. All measurements
include a $\frac{1}{4}$" seam allowance. Sew
with right sides together unless
otherwise stated.

Design: Joy Hoffman
Photographs: Marcia Cameron

Cut the Fabrics

To make the best use of your fabrics, cut
the pieces in the order that follows. The
patterns are on *page 38*. To make
templates of the patterns, follow the
instructions in Quilting Basics, which
begins on *page 91*.

From light blue print, cut:
• 18—$2\frac{1}{2}$×$6\frac{1}{2}$" rectangles
• 27—$2\frac{1}{2}$" squares
• 21—$1\frac{1}{2}$×$2\frac{1}{2}$" rectangles
• 21 of Pattern A
• 9 *each* of patterns B and B reversed
• 3—$4\frac{1}{2}$×$8\frac{1}{2}$" rectangles
• 3—$4\frac{1}{2}$" squares
From white print, cut:
• 9 *each* of patterns B and B reversed
• 2—$2\frac{1}{2}$×$36\frac{1}{2}$" inner border strips
• 2—$2\frac{1}{2}$×$32\frac{1}{2}$" inner border strips
From red print, cut:
• 9 of Pattern A
• 9—$2\frac{1}{2}$×$8\frac{1}{2}$" rectangles
• 2—$1\frac{1}{2}$×$40\frac{1}{2}$" middle border strips
• 2—$1\frac{1}{2}$×$36\frac{1}{2}$" middle border strips
From blue print, cut:
• 24 *each* of patterns B and B reversed
From dark blue print No. 1, cut:
• 5—$2\frac{1}{2}$×42" binding strips
• 2—$2\frac{1}{2}$×$42\frac{1}{2}$" outer border strips
• 2—$2\frac{1}{2}$×$38\frac{1}{2}$" outer border strips
• 9 *each* of patterns B and B reversed
From dark blue print No. 2, cut:
• 9 *each* of patterns B and B reversed
From dark blue print No. 3, cut:
• 6 *each* of patterns B and B reversed
From light gold print, cut:
• 6 of Pattern A
From dark gold print, cut:
• 6 of Pattern A
• 8—$2\frac{1}{2}$" squares
• 4—$1\frac{1}{2}$" squares
• 9—1×$4\frac{1}{2}$" rectangles

Assemble the Star Blocks

1. For one star block you'll need two
light gold print A triangles, two dark
gold print A triangles, four light blue
print A triangles, and four light blue print
$1\frac{1}{2}$×$2\frac{1}{2}$" rectangles.

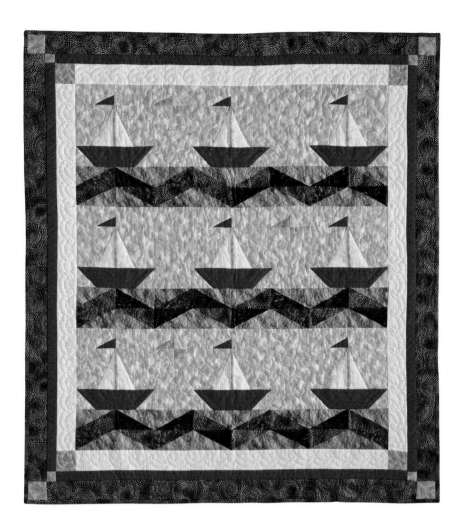

direction with the row. Then join the rows to make a star block. Press the seam allowance open. The pieced star block should measure 4½" square, including the seam allowances.

Diagram 3

6. Repeat steps 1 through 5 to make a total of three star blocks.

Assemble the Boat Blocks

1. For one boat block you'll need three light blue print 2½" squares, two light blue print 2½×6½" rectangles, one light blue print 1½×2½" rectangle, one light blue print A triangle, one light blue print B triangle, one light blue print B reversed triangle, one white print B triangle, one white print B reversed triangle, one dark gold print 1×4½" rectangle, one red print A triangle, and one red print 2½×8½" rectangle.

2. Referring to Diagram 4 for placement, sew together the red print A triangle and the light blue print A triangle to make the flag rectangle. Press the seam allowance toward the red print triangle. Sew the light blue print 1½×2½" rectangle to the light blue long edge of the flag rectangle. Then add a light blue print 2½" square to the red-and-blue edge to complete the flag unit. Press the seam allowances in one direction.

Diagram 4

3. Sew together a light blue print B triangle and a white print B triangle to make a mast rectangle (see Diagram 5).

2. Sew together a light gold print A triangle and a light blue print A triangle to make a star point (see Diagram 1). Press the seam allowance toward the light gold print triangle. Repeat with the second light gold print triangle and a second light blue print triangle.

Diagram 1

3. Pair the two dark gold print A triangles with the remaining two light blue print triangles. Sew together as in Step 2 to make a total of four star points.

4. Sew a light blue print 1½×2½" rectangle to the light blue long edge of each star point (see Diagram 2) to make four star point units. Press the seam allowances toward the light blue print rectangles.

Diagram 2

5. Referring to Diagram 3 for placement, lay out the four star point units in two horizontal rows. Sew together the units in each row. Press the seam allowance in each row in one direction, alternating the

Press the seam allowance toward the light blue print triangle. Repeat with the light blue print B reversed triangle and the white print B reversed triangle. Press the seam allowance toward the white print triangle.

Diagram 5

4. Sew mast rectangles to the long edges of the dark gold print 1×4½" rectangle to make the mast unit (see Diagram 6). Press the seam allowances toward the mast rectangles.

Diagram 6

5. With wrong sides together, fold the mast unit in half (see Diagram 7). Sew the long edges of the dark gold print rectangle together, sewing in the ditch. Open up the mast unit (see Diagram 8). Press the dark gold print strip flat to create a three-dimensional mast unit.

Diagram 7   Diagram 8

6. Sew the flag unit to the top edge of the mast unit (see Diagram 9). Press the seam allowance toward the flag unit. Sew light blue print 2½×6½" rectangles to the long edges of the flag-and-mast unit. Press the seam allowances toward the light blue print rectangles.

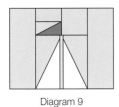

Diagram 9

7. Use a pencil to make a diagonal line on the wrong side of the two remaining light blue 2½" squares for accurate sewing lines. (To prevent your fabric from stretching as you draw the lines, place 220-grit sandpaper under the squares.)

8. Align a marked light blue print square with one end of the red print 2½×8½" rectangle (see Diagram 10; note the placement of the marked diagonal line). Stitch on the marked line; trim the seam allowance to ¼". Press the attached triangle open.

9. Align the second marked light blue print square with the opposite end of the

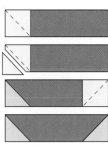

Diagram 10

red print rectangle (see Diagram 10, again noting the placement of the marked diagonal line). Stitch on the marked line; trim and press as before to complete the boat unit.

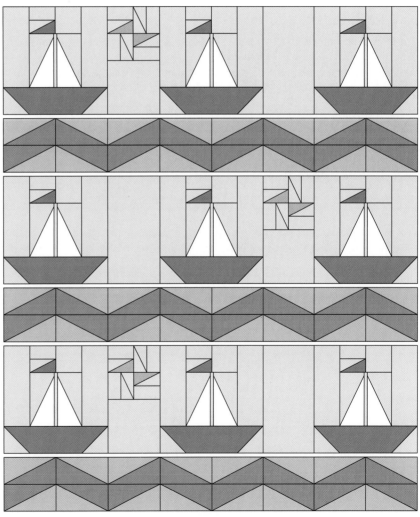

Quilt Assembly Diagram

10. Sew the boat unit to the bottom edge of the flag-and-mast unit to complete the boat block. Press the seam allowance toward the boat unit. The pieced boat block should measure $8\frac{1}{2}$" square, including the seam allowances.

11. Repeat steps 1 through 10 to make a total of nine boat blocks.

Assemble the Sashing Units

1. Referring to Diagram 11 for placement, pair the 48 blue print B and B reversed triangles with the 48 dark blue print B or B reversed triangles.

Diagram 11

2. Sew the paired triangles together to make a total of 48 sashing units. Press the seam allowances in the B pairs toward the blue print triangles and in the B reversed pairs toward the dark blue print triangles.

Assemble the Quilt Center

1. Referring to the Quilt Assembly Diagram on *page 37* for placement, lay out the boat blocks, star blocks, sashing units, light blue print $4\frac{1}{2}$" squares, and light blue print $4\frac{1}{2}\times8\frac{1}{2}$" rectangles in rows. Sew together the pieces in each row. Press the seam allowances in one direction, alternating the direction in each row.

2. Then join the rows. The pieced quilt center should measure $32\frac{1}{2}\times36\frac{1}{2}$", including the seam allowances.

Add the Borders

1. Sew the white print $2\frac{1}{2}\times32\frac{1}{2}$" inner border strips to the top and bottom edges of the pieced quilt center. Sew a dark gold print $2\frac{1}{2}$" square to each end of the white print $2\frac{1}{2}\times36\frac{1}{2}$" inner border strips. Sew the pieced strips to the side edges of the pieced quilt center. Press all seam allowances toward the white-on-white border.

2. Sew the red print $1\frac{1}{2}\times36\frac{1}{2}$" middle border strips to the top and bottom edges of the pieced quilt center. Sew a dark gold print $1\frac{1}{2}$" square to each end of the red print $1\frac{1}{2}\times40\frac{1}{2}$" middle border strips. Sew the pieced strips to the side edges of the pieced quilt center. Press all seam allowances toward the red print border.

3. Sew the dark blue print $2\frac{1}{2}\times38\frac{1}{2}$" outer border strips to the top and bottom edges of the pieced quilt center. Sew a dark gold print $2\frac{1}{2}$" square to each end of the dark blue print $2\frac{1}{2}\times42\frac{1}{2}$" outer border strips. Sew the pieced strip to the side edges of the pieced quilt center. Press all seam allowances toward the dark blue border.

Complete the Quilt

1. Layer the quilt top, batting, and backing according to the instructions in Quilting Basics, which begins on *page 91*. Quilt as desired.

2. Use the dark blue print $2\frac{1}{2}\times42$" strips to bind the quilt according to the instructions in Quilting Basics.

patterns

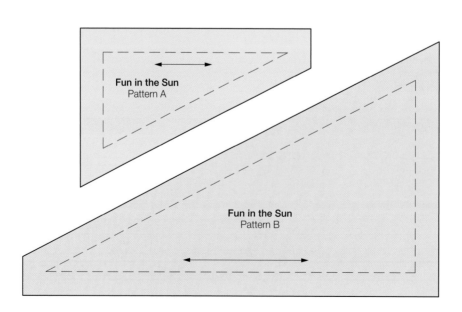

cherry ORCHARD

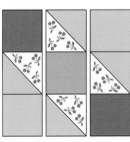

Taste buds WILL TINGLE WHEN THIS ORCHARD WORKS ITS WAY INTO YOUR KITCHEN. FIND FABRIC OF YOUR FAVORITE FRUIT—AND HAVE SOME FLAVORFUL FUN.

Materials

⅞ yard of floral cherry print for blocks, outer border, and binding
¼ yard of green print for blocks and inner border
⅜ yard of light green print for blocks
¼ yard of red print for blocks
½ yard of cherry branch print for setting squares
1¼ yards of backing fabric
42" square of quilt batting

Finished quilt top: 36" square
Finished block: 6" square

Quantities specified for 44/45"-wide, 100% cotton fabrics. All measurements include a ¼" seam allowance. Sew with right sides together unless otherwise stated.

Design: Margaret Rouleau
Photograph: Craig Anderson

Cut the Fabrics

To make the best use of your fabrics, cut the pieces in the order that follows.

From floral cherry print, cut:
• 4—2½×42" binding strips
• 4—3×39" outer border strips
• 26—2⅞" squares

From green print, cut:
• 4—1×33" inner border strips
• 13—2½" squares

From light green print, cut:
• 26—2⅞" squares
• 26—2½" squares

From red print, cut:
• 26—2½" squares

From cherry branch print, cut:
• 12—6½" squares

Assemble the Blocks

1. Use a quilter's pencil to mark a diagonal line on the wrong side of the light green print 2⅞" squares. (To prevent the fabric from stretching as you draw the lines, place 220-grit sandpaper under the squares.)

2. Layer each marked light green print 2⅞" square atop a floral cherry print 2⅞" square. Sew each pair together with two seams, stitching ¼" on each side of the drawn line (see Diagram 1).

3. Cut each pair apart on its drawn line to make two triangle units each. Press each triangle unit open to make a triangle-square. Each triangle-square should measure 2½" square, including the seam allowances. You should have a total of 52 triangle-squares.

Diagram 1

4. Referring to Diagram 2 for placement, lay out four triangle-squares, two red print 2½" squares, two light green print 2½" squares, and one green print 2½" square in three vertical rows.

5. Sew together the squares in each row. Press the seam allowances away from the triangle-squares. Then join the rows to make a pieced block. Press the seam allowances in one direction. The pieced block should measure 6½" square, including the seam allowances.

6. Repeat steps 4 and 5 to make a total of 13 pieced blocks.

Assemble the Quilt Center

1. Referring to the photograph *opposite* for placement, lay out the 13 pieced blocks and the 12 cherry branch print 6½" squares in five horizontal rows.

2. Sew together the squares in each row. Press the seam allowances toward the cherry branch print setting squares. Join the rows to make the quilt center. Press the seam allowances in one direction. The pieced quilt center should measure 30½" square, including the seam allowances.

Add the Borders

1. Matching the centers and aligning long edges, sew together a floral cherry print 3×39" outer border strip and a green print 1×33" inner border strip to make a border unit. Repeat to make a total of four border units.

2. Add the border units to the quilt center, mitering the corners, to complete the quilt top. For instructions on mitering, see Quilting Basics, which begins on *page 91*.

Complete the Quilt

1. Layer the quilt top, batting, and backing according to the instructions in Quilting Basics. Quilt as desired.

2. Use the floral cherry print 2½×42" strips to bind the quilt according to the instructions in Quilting Basics.

REVERSIBLE ROUND TABLECLOTH

Materials
4 yards of floral cherry print
4 yards of cherry branch print

Finished tablecloth: 70" diameter

Cut the Fabrics
From floral cherry print, cut:
• 2—42×72" panels
From cherry branch print, cut:
• 2—42×72" panels

Assemble the Tablecloth

1. Cut one floral cherry print 42×72" panel in half lengthwise to make two 21×72" rectangles. *Note*: As with quilted projects, be sure to cut off the selvages. Sew the two small rectangles to the side edges of the remaining floral cherry print piece (see Diagram 3). Press the seam allowances toward the center rectangle. The pieced floral cherry tablecloth top should measure 72×83", including the seam allowances.

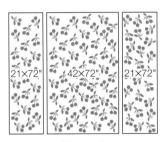

Diagram 3

2. Repeat Step 1 using the cherry branch print pieces to make a pieced cherry branch print tablecloth top. Press the seam allowances away from the center rectangle.

3. Referring to Diagram 4, fold the floral cherry print tablecloth top into quarters, right sides together. Using a large compass, mark a 35¼" radius. (Or, insert a straight pin through a tape measure and push the pin through the center corner fold. Rotate the tape measure to mark the

35¼" radius, using a quilter's marking pencil.) Cut along the marked line to make a 70½" diameter circle.

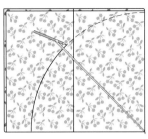

Diagram 4

4. Repeat Step 3 using the cherry branch print tablecloth top.

5. Place the two tablecloth top circles together, pinning edges frequently as you will be sewing on the bias. Sew together, leaving a 6" opening for turning. Turn the tablecloth right side out and hand-stitch the opening closed; press.

DINNER NAPKINS

Materials for Four Napkins
1 yard of floral cherry print
1 yard of green print

Finished napkin: 17" square

Cut the Fabrics
From floral cherry print, cut:
• 4—17½" squares
From green print, cut:
• 4—17½" squares

Assemble the Napkins

1. Sew together a floral cherry print and a green print square, leaving a 4" opening for turning. Turn the napkin right side out and hand-stitch the opening closed; press.

2. Repeat to make a total of four napkins.

Note: To make luncheon-size napkins, you'll need ⅞ yard of each fabric. Cut the fabric into 14½" squares and sew as for the dinner napkins. The finished napkins will be 14" square.

watermelon PATCH

THIS *picnic cloth* SHOULD BE MADE OF WASHABLE FABRIC. HOPEFULLY, IT WILL BE BLESSED WITH LOTS OF SUMMER SPILLS AND WATERMELON SEEDS.

Materials

½ yard of red print for watermelon, dogtooth border, and outer border
⅜ yard of beige print for background
⅜ yard of green print for watermelon rind, dogtooth border, and border corners
¼ yard of dark green print for binding
⅞ yard of backing fabric
30" square of quilt batting

Finished quilt top: 24" square

Quantities specified for 44/45"-wide, 100% cotton fabrics. All measurements include a ¼" seam allowance. Sew with right sides together unless otherwise stated.

Design: Lynette Jensen
Photograph: Perry Struse

Cut the Fabrics

To make the best use of your fabrics, cut the pieces in the order that follows.

From red print, cut:
- 5—4⅜" squares, cutting each in half diagonally for a total of 10 triangles (you'll have 1 leftover triangle)
- 4—3½×16½" strips for outer border
- 64—1½" squares

From beige print, cut:
- 5—4⅜" squares, cutting each in half diagonally for a total of 10 triangles (you'll have 1 leftover triangle)

- 2—1½×16½" sashing strips
- 4—1½×14½" sashing strips
- 6—1½×4½" sashing strips

From green print, cut:
- 4—4½" squares
- 32—1½×2½" rectangles
- 9—1×4½" rectangles
- 9—1×4" rectangles

From dark green print, cut:
- 3—2½×42" binding strips

Assemble the Watermelon Blocks

1. Join a beige print triangle and a red print triangle to make a triangle-square (see Diagram 1). Press the seam allowance toward the red print triangle. The pieced triangle-square should measure 4" square, including the seam allowances.

Diagram 1

2. Referring to Diagram 2 on *page 44* for placement, sew a green print 1×4" rectangle to the bottom edge of the triangle-square. Press the seam allowance toward the green print rectangle. Sew a green print 1×4½" rectangle to the left edge of the triangle-square to make a watermelon block. Press the seam allowance toward the green print rectangle. The pieced watermelon block

should measure 4½" square, including the seam allowances. Repeat to make a total of nine watermelon blocks.

Diagram 2

Assemble the Quilt Center

1. Referring to the photograph *below right* for placement, lay out the nine watermelon blocks, the six beige print 1½×4½" sashing strips, and the four beige print 1½×14½" sashing strips in seven vertical rows.

2. Sew together the pieces in each block row. Press the seam allowances toward the sashing strips. Then join the rows. Add a beige print 1½×16½" sashing strip to the top and bottom edges of the pieced rows to complete the quilt center. Press the seam allowances in one direction. The pieced quilt center should measure 16½" square, including the seam allowances.

Assemble and Add the Borders

1. Using a quilter's pencil, mark a diagonal line on the wrong side of the 64 red print 1½" squares.

2. Align a marked red print 1½" square with one end of a green print 1½×2½" rectangle (see Diagram 3; note the placement of the marked diagonal line). Stitch on the marked line; trim the seam allowance to ¼". Press the attached triangle open. Align a second marked red print 1½" square with the opposite end of the green print rectangle (see Diagram 3, again noting the placement of the marked line); stitch, trim, and press as before to make a dogtooth unit.

Diagram 3

The pieced dogtooth unit should still measure 1½×2½", including the seam allowances. Repeat to make a total of 32 dogtooth units.

3. Referring to Diagram 4 for placement, sew together eight dogtooth units to make a dogtooth border strip. Press the seam allowances in one direction. The pieced border strip should measure 1½×16½", including the seam allowances. Repeat to make a total of four dogtooth border strips.

Diagram 4

4. Referring to the photograph *below* for placement, sew the pieced dogtooth border strips to the red print 3½×16½" border strips to make four pieced outer border strips. Press the seam allowances toward the red print border.

5. Sew the pieced outer border strips to opposite edges of the pieced quilt center. Sew a green print 4½" square to each end of the remaining pieced outer border strips. Press the seam allowances toward the pieced outer border. Add the pieced outer border strips to the remaining edges of the pieced quilt center to complete the quilt top. Press the seam allowances toward the pieced outer border.

Complete the Quilt

1. Layer the quilt top, batting, and backing according to the instructions in Quilting Basics, which begins on *page 91*. Quilt as desired.

2. Use the dark green print 2½×42" strips to bind the quilt according to the instructions in Quilting Basics.

autumn apples
PILLOW

IT'S A LOT EASIER THAN GROWING GOOD APPLES: USING FREEZER PAPER, YOU IRON ON THE MOTIFS, THEN HAND-STITCH AROUND THEM FOR *fine folk art* CHARM.

Materials

1⅛ yards of pale gold print for appliqué
   foundation and pillow back
¼ yard of light brown print for twig
   appliqués and inner border
2—⅛-yard pieces of assorted gold prints
   for pieced outer border
⅛ yard of red print for apple appliqués
⅛ yard of green print for leaf appliqués
24" square of muslin for pillow top lining
24" square of quilt batting
18" square pillow form
Freezer paper

Finished pillow: 18" square

Quantities specified for 44/45"-wide,
100% cotton fabrics. All measurements
include a ¼" seam allowance. Sew
with right sides together unless
otherwise stated.

Design: Kris Kerrigan
Photograph: Perry Struse

Cut the Fabrics

To make the best use of your fabrics, cut
the pieces in the order that follows. The
patterns are *below*. To use freezer paper
for appliquéing, as was done in this
project, complete the following steps.

1. Lay the freezer paper, shiny side down,
over the patterns. Use a pencil to trace
each pattern the number of times
indicated, leaving a ¼" space between
tracings. Cut out each piece on the
traced lines.

2. Press the freezer-paper shapes onto the
wrong sides of the designated fabrics,
leaving ½" between shapes; let cool. Cut
out fabric shapes roughly ³/16" beyond
the freezer-paper edges.

3. Finger-press the seam allowances
around the edges of the freezer-paper
shapes.

From pale gold print, cut:
• 2—18½×24" rectangles for pillow back
• 1—15½" square for appliqué
   foundation
From light brown print, cut:
• 4—1×19" inner border strips
• 4—1¼×8" bias strips for twig
   appliqués
From each of the assorted gold prints, cut:
• 4—19"-long strips that are ½"-wide at
   one end and 1½"-wide at the opposite
   end for outer border strips (see
   Diagram 1)

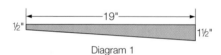

Diagram 1

From red print, cut:
• 4 of Pattern A
From green print, cut:
• 4 *each* of patterns B and B reversed
• 8 *each* of patterns C and D

Prepare the Twig Appliqués

1. Fold a light brown print 1¼×8"
bias strip in half lengthwise with the
wrong side inside. Using a ⅛" seam
allowance, sew the length of the strip
(see Diagram 2).

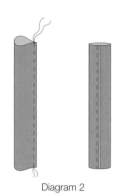

Diagram 2

2. Roll the strip so that the seam is in the
middle of one side; press flat. Fold under
one of the ends at an angle and press to
make a twig appliqué. Repeat to make a
total of four twig appliqués.

Appliqué the Pillow Top

1. To ensure precise appliqué placement
lines, fold the pale gold print 15½"
square appliqué foundation in half
diagonally and press the folded edge.
Unfold the square. Fold it in half
diagonally in the opposite direction;
press, then unfold.

patterns

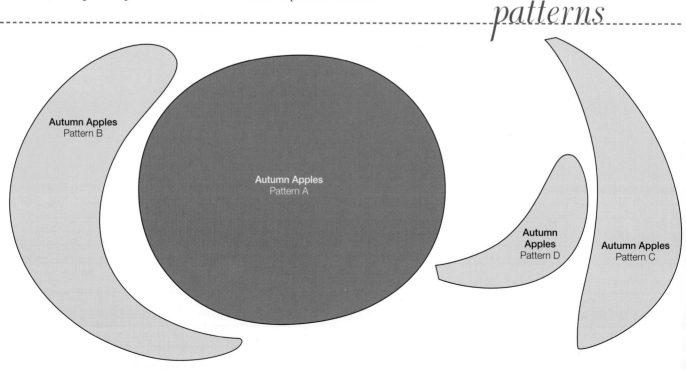

Autumn Apples
Pattern B

Autumn Apples
Pattern A

Autumn Apples
Pattern D

Autumn Apples
Pattern C

2. Referring to the photograph on *page 45* for placement, arrange the prepared twig appliqués on the appliqué foundation using the fold lines as positioning guides; baste in place. Using light brown thread, appliqué the twigs in place.

3. Position the prepared leaf and apple appliqués on the appliqué foundation; baste in place.

4. Using small slip stitches and threads that match the fabrics, appliqué the pieces in place, leaving a ½" opening in each. Using the openings for access, remove the freezer paper shapes by sliding your needle between the fabric and freezer paper. Gently loosen and pull out the freezer paper. Slip-stitch the openings closed to finish the pillow center.

Assemble and Add the Border

1. With right sides together, sew together two contrasting gold print angled 19"-long border strips (see Diagram 3). Press the seam allowance in one direction. The pieced border strip should measure 1½×19", including the seam allowances. Repeat to make a total of four border strips.

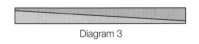

Diagram 3

2. Join a light brown 1×19" inner border strip to a pieced gold print border strip to make a border unit; press. The pieced border unit should measure 2×19", including the seam allowances. Repeat to make a total of four pieced border units.

3. With midpoints aligned, pin a pieced 2×19" border unit to each edge of the appliquéd pillow center; allow excess border fabric to extend beyond the edges. Sew each border unit to the pillow center, beginning and ending the seam ¼" from the corners (see Diagram 4). Press the seam allowances toward the border.

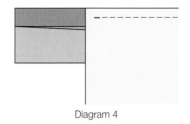

Diagram 4

4. Miter the border corners to complete the pillow top.

To miter a border corner, overlap the border strips at each corner. Align the edge of a 90° right triangle with the raw edge of the border strip on the top so that the long edge of the triangle intersects the seam in the corner (see Diagram 5); mark the diagonal line. Place the bottom border strip on top and repeat the marking process.

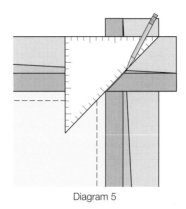

Diagram 5

With right sides together, match the marked seam lines and pin (see Diagram 6).

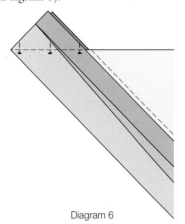

Diagram 6

Beginning with a backstitch at the inside corner, stitch exactly on the marked lines to the raw edges of the border strips. Check the right side of the corner to see that it lies flat. Then trim the excess fabric, leaving a ¼" seam allowance. Press the seam open.

Quilt the Pillow Top

Layer the pieced pillow top, batting, and muslin 24" square according to the instructions in Quilting Basics, which begins on *page 91*. Quilt as desired.

Assemble the Pillow Back

1. With wrong sides inside, fold the two pale gold 18½×24" rectangles in half to form two 12×18½" double-thick pillow back pieces.

2. Referring to Diagram 7 for placement, overlap the two folded edges by about 4"; stitch the pieces in place, sewing across the folds, to create a single pillow back.

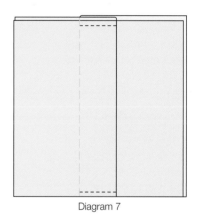

Diagram 7

3. With right sides together, layer the quilted pillow top and the pillow back; pin. Sew together around the outer edges to make the pillow cover. Turn the pillow cover right side out; press.

4. Insert the pillow form through the back opening to complete the pillow.

Queen Ann's COURT

Materials

2½ yards of cream print for background
1 yard of purple print for blocks
2⅝ yards of leaf print for blocks and
    inner border
2⅝ yards of gold print for blocks and
    middle border
2⅝ yards of green floral for blocks,
    outer border, and binding
4½ yards of backing fabric
81" square of quilt batting

Finished quilt top: 75" square
Finished block: 15" square

Quantities specified for 44/45"-wide,
100% cotton fabrics. All measurements
include a ¼" seam allowance. Sew
with right sides together unless
otherwise stated.

Design: Ginny King
Photographs: Perry Struse

Cut the Fabrics

To make the best use of your fabrics, cut
the pieces in the order that follows. The
border strips are cut longer than specified
to allow for mitering the corners. The
border strips are cut the length of the
fabric (parallel to the selvage).

From cream print, cut:
• 128—3⅞" squares, cutting each in half
    diagonally for a total of 256 triangles
• 96—3½" squares

From purple print, cut:
• 32—3⅞" squares, cutting each in half
    diagonally for a total of 64 triangles
• 32—3½" squares

From leaf print, cut:
• 4—3×90" strips for inner border
• 32—3⅞" squares, cutting each in half
    diagonally for a total of 64 triangles
• 16—3½" squares

From gold print, cut:
• 4—2×90" strips for middle border
• 32—3⅞" squares, cutting each in half
    diagonally for a total of 64 triangles

From green floral, cut:
• 4—4×90" strips for outside border
• 8—2½×42" binding strips
• 32—3⅞" squares, cutting each in half
    diagonally for a total of 64 triangles

Assemble the Blocks

1. For one block you'll need 16 cream
print triangles, six cream print squares,
four purple print triangles, two purple
print squares, one leaf print square, four
leaf print triangles, four gold print
triangles, and four green floral triangles.

2. Sew a cream print triangle to a triangle
of another color to make a triangle-
square. Press the seam allowance toward
the darker triangle. The triangle-square
should measure 3½" square, including
the seam allowances. Repeat to make
a total of 16 triangle-squares (see
Diagram 1).

Diagram 1

3. Referring to Diagram 2 for placement,
lay out all the squares and triangle-
squares in five horizontal rows of five
squares or triangle-squares each.

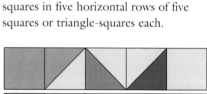

Diagram 2

4. Sew together the squares and triangle-
squares in each row. Press the seam
allowances in each row in one direction,
alternating the direction with each row.
Then join the rows to make a Queen's
Crown block. Press the seam allowances
in one direction. The pieced block should
measure 15½" square, including the
seam allowances.

5. Repeat steps 1 through 4 to make a
total of 16 Queen's Crown blocks.

WITH THE LARGE *triangles* AND *squares* FOUND
IN THIS REGAL QUILT, IT'S THE PERFECT SPOT TO
HIGHLIGHT A LARGE FLORAL PRINT.

Assemble the Quilt Center

1. Referring to the photograph *opposite* and the Quilt Assembly Diagram *below*, lay out the blocks in four horizontal rows of four blocks each. To create a secondary star design, make sure like green floral triangles are positioned together to form the stars.

2. Sew together the blocks in each row. Press the seam allowances in each row in one direction, alternating the direction with each row. Then join the rows to make the quilt center. The pieced quilt center should measure 60½" square, including the seam allowances.

Add the Borders

1. For each border you'll need one leaf print 3×90" strip, one gold print 2×90" strip, and one green floral 4×90" strip. Aligning the long raw edges, join the strips to make a border strip. Repeat to make a total of four border strips.

2. To add the border with mitered corners, first pin a border strip to the quilt center edge, matching the center of the strip and the center of the quilt top

edge. Sew together, beginning and ending the seam ¼" from the quilt top corners (see Diagram 3). Allow excess border fabric to extend beyond the edges. Repeat with remaining border strips. Press the seam allowances toward the border strips.

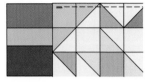

Diagram 3

3. At one corner, lap one border strip over the other (see Diagram 4). Align the edge of a 90° right triangle with the raw

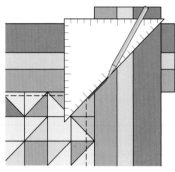

Diagram 4

edge of the top strip so the long edge of the triangle intersects the border seam in the corner. With a pencil, draw along the edge of the triangle from the seam out to the raw edge. Place the bottom border strip on top and repeat the marking process.

4. With the right sides together, match the marked seam lines and pin (see Diagram 5).

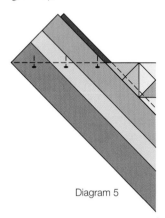

Diagram 5

5. Beginning with a backstitch at the quilt top edge, sew together the strips, stitching exactly on the marked lines. Check the right side to see that the corner lies flat. Trim the excess fabric, leaving a ¼" seam allowance. Press the seam open. Mark and sew the remaining corners in the same manner.

Complete the Quilt

1. Layer the quilt top, batting, and backing according to the instructions in Quilting Basics, which begins on page *91*. Quilt as desired.

2. Use the green floral 2½×42" strips to bind the quilt according to the instructions in Quilting Basics.

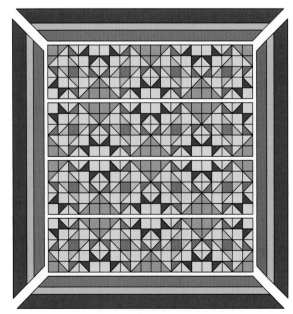

Quilt Assembly Diagram

STARS OF *friendship* AMID TOWERING TREES — WITH NINE-PATCH BLOCKS TO TIE IT ALL TOGETHER: YOU'LL ENJOY "GROWING" THIS QUILT AS MUCH AS ANY GARDEN.

BOUNTIFUL *harvest*

Materials

2¾ yards of beige print for star, Nine-Patch, and leaf blocks

½ yard of gold print for star blocks

1 yard of purple print for Nine-Patch blocks, inner border, and narrow middle border

4—¼-yard pieces of assorted orange and brown prints for Nine-Patch blocks

6—⅛-yard pieces of assorted russet and chestnut prints for Nine-Patch blocks

5—¼-yard pieces of assorted green prints for leaf blocks

1⅜ yards of black print for wide middle border and binding

1½ yards of dark brown print for outer border

5⅛ yards of backing fabric

80×92" of quilt batting

Finished quilt top: 74×86"
Finished blocks: 6" square

Quantities specified for 44/45"-wide, 100% cotton fabrics. All measurements include a ¼" seam allowance. Sew with right sides together unless otherwise stated.

Design: Lynette Jensen
Photographs: Perry Struse; Steve Struse

Cut the Fabrics

To make the best use of your fabrics, cut the pieces in the order that follows.

From beige print, cut:
- 15—2½×42" strips
- 30—2⅝" squares, cutting each in half diagonally for a total of 60 triangles
- 196—2½" squares
- 38—2½×4½" rectangles

From gold print, cut:
- 19—2½×6½" rectangles
- 38—2½" squares

From purple print, cut:
- 4—2½×42" strips
- 7—1½×42" strips for inner border
- 8—1½×42" strips for narrow middle border

From each assorted orange and brown print, cut:
- 2—2½×42" strips

From each assorted russet and chestnut print, cut:
- 1—2½×42" strip

From each assorted green print, cut:
- 6—4½" squares
- 12—2½×4½" rectangles
- 6—1×5" strips

From black print, cut:
- 7—3½×42" strips for wide middle border
- 8—2½×42" binding strips

From dark brown print, cut:
- 9—5½×42" strips for outer border

Assemble the Star Blocks

1. For accurate sewing lines, use a quilter's pencil to mark a diagonal line on the wrong side of two beige print 2½" squares and two gold print 2½" squares. (To prevent your fabric from stretching as you draw the lines, place 220-grit sandpaper under the squares.)

2. With right sides together, align a marked beige print 2½" square with each end of a gold print 2½×6½" rectangle (see Diagram 1; note the placement of the marked diagonal lines). Stitch on the marked lines; trim the seam allowances to ¼". Press the attached triangles open.

Diagram 1

3. With right sides together, align a gold print 2½" square with the right end of a beige print 2½×4½" rectangle (see Diagram 2; note the placement of the marked diagonal line). Stitch on the marked line; trim the seam allowance to ¼". Press the attached triangle open. Sew an unmarked beige print 2½" square to the right short edge of the rectangle to make a star point unit (see Diagram 3).

Diagram 2

Diagram 3

4. Repeat Step 3 to make a total of two star point units.

5. Lay out the unit made in Step 2 and two star point units as shown in Diagram 4. Sew together the rows to make a star block. Press the seam allowances in one direction. The star block should measure 6½" square, including the seam allowances.

Diagram 4

6. Repeat steps 1 through 5 to make a total of 19 star blocks.

Assemble the Nine-Patch Blocks

1. Aligning long raw edges, sew together one purple print 2½×42" strip and two beige print 2½×42" strips to make a strip set A (see Diagram 5). Press the seam allowances toward the purple print strip. Repeat to make a total of four of strip set A.

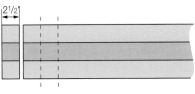

Diagram 5

2. Cut the four strip sets into 2½"-wide segments for a total of 50.

3. In the same manner, sew one of the assorted orange, brown, russet, or chestnut print 2½×42" strips to each long edge of a beige print 2½×42" strip to make a strip set B (see Diagram 6). Press the seam allowances toward the dark strips. Repeat to make a total of seven of strip set B.

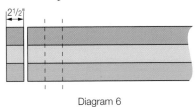

Diagram 6

4. Cut the seven strip sets into 2½"-wide segments for a total of 100.

5. Lay out one strip set A segment and two strip set B segments as shown in Diagram 7. Sew together the rows to make a Nine-Patch block. Press the seam allowances in one direction. The Nine-Patch block should measure 6½" square, including the seam allowances.

Diagram 7

6. Repeat Step 5 for a total of 50 Nine-Patch blocks.

Assemble the Leaf Blocks

1. For accurate sewing lines, use a quilter's pencil to mark a diagonal line on the wrong side of the four beige print 2½" squares.

2. With right sides together, align a marked beige print 2½" square with opposite corners of a green print 4½" square (see Diagram 8; note the placement of the marked diagonal lines). Stitch on the marked lines; trim the seam allowances to ¼". Press the attached triangles open.

Diagram 8

3. With right sides together, align a marked beige print 2½" square with the right end of a green print 2½×4½" rectangle (see Diagram 9; note the placement of the marked diagonal line). Stitch on the marked line; trim the seam allowance to ¼". Press the attached triangle open.

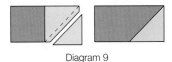

Diagram 9

4. Repeat Step 3, but with the diagonal line running the opposite direction (see Diagram 10).

Diagram 10

5. Aligning long edges, sew together the green print 1×5" strip and one beige print triangle (see Diagram 11). Join a second beige print right triangle to the opposite long edge of the strip to complete the stem unit. Press the seam allowances toward the green print strip. Trim the pieced stem unit so it measures 2½" square, including the seam allowances.

Diagram 11

6. Referring to Diagram 12, lay out the four units in two horizontal rows. Sew together the pieces in each row. Press the seam allowances in opposite directions. Then join the rows to make a leaf block. Press the seam allowances in one direction. The leaf block should measure 6½" square, including the seam allowances.

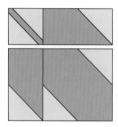

Diagram 12

7. Repeat steps 1 through 6 to make six leaf blocks from each of the five green prints for a total of 30 leaf blocks.

Assemble the Quilt Center
Referring to the photograph on *page 54* for placement, lay out the star, Nine-Patch, and leaf blocks in 11 horizontal rows of nine blocks each. Sew together the blocks in each horizontal row. Then join the rows. The pieced quilt center should measure 54½×66½", including the seam allowances.

Add the Borders
The following instructions include the mathematically correct border strip lengths for this quilt. Measure your pieced quilt center and adjust the border strip lengths accordingly.

1. Cut and piece the purple print 1½×42" strips to make the following:
- 2—1½×54½" inner border strips
- 2—1½×68½" inner border strips
- 2—1½×62½" narrow middle border strips
- 2—1½×76½" narrow middle border strips

2. Sew one purple print 1½×54½" inner border strip to the top and bottom edges of the pieced quilt center. Then add a purple print 1½×68½" inner border strip to each side edge of the pieced quilt center. Press the seam allowances toward the purple print border.

3. Cut and piece the black print 3½×42" strips to make the following:
- 2—3½×56½" wide middle border strips
- 2—3½×74½" wide middle border strips

4. Sew one black print 3½×56½" wide middle border strip to the top and bottom edges of the pieced quilt center.

Then add a black print 3½×74½" wide middle border strip to each side edge of the pieced quilt center. Press the seam allowances toward the black print border.

5. Sew one purple print 1½×62½" narrow middle border strip to the top and bottom edges of the pieced quilt center. Then add a purple print 1½×76½" narrow middle border strip to each side edge of the pieced quilt center. Press the seam allowances toward the purple print middle border.

6. Cut and piece the dark brown print 5½×42" strips to make the following:
- 2—5½×64½" outer border strips
- 2—5½×86½" outer border strips

7. Sew one dark brown print 5½×64½" outer border strip to the top and bottom edges of the pieced quilt center. Then add a dark brown print 5½×86½" outer border strip to each side edge of the pieced quilt center to complete the quilt top. Press the seam allowances toward the brown print border.

Complete the Quilt
1. Layer the quilt top, batting, and backing according to the instructions in Quilting Basics, which begins on *page 91*. Quilt as desired.

2. Use the black print 2½×42" strips to bind the quilt according to the instructions in Quilting Basics.

SIMPLE *Joys*

ADD *homespun happiness* TO YOUR HOLIDAYS WITH TWO TRADITIONAL BLOCKS AND HAND-DYED FABRICS. ADD BUTTONS THAT CELEBRATE YOUR TRADITIONS.

Materials

1 yard of solid red for hearts and stars
1 yard of solid green for Puss in the Corner blocks, narrow border, and binding
1¼ yards of parchment print for block background
1 yard of red-and-green plaid for borders
51" square of backing fabric
51" square of quilt batting
9 Santa buttons
8 *each* of two tree-shape buttons

Finished quilt top: 45" square
Finished star block: 6" square
Finished Puss in the Corner block: 6" square
Finished heart block: 5" square

Quantities specified for 44/45"–wide, 100% cotton fabrics. All measurements include a ¼" seam allowance. Sew with right sides together unless otherwise stated.

Design: Sylvia Johnson
Photographs: Perry Struse

Cut the Fabrics

To make the best use of your fabrics, cut the pieces in the order that follows. The Heart Pattern is on *page 60.* To make a template of the pattern, follow the instructions in Quilting Basics, which begins on *page 91.*

From solid red, cut:
• 16—3½" squares for star centers
• 128—2" squares for star points
• 4 of Heart Pattern
From solid green, cut:
• 5—2½×42" binding strips
• 2—1×35½" inner border strips
• 2—1×34½" inner border strips
• 9—3½" squares
• 36—2" squares
From parchment print, cut:
• 3—9¾" squares, cutting each diagonally twice in an X for a total of 12 side triangles
• 4—5½" squares
• 2—5⅛" squares, cutting each in half diagonally for a total of 4 corner triangles
• 100—2×3½" rectangles
• 64— 2" squares
From red-and-green plaid, cut:
• 4—5½×35½" outer border strips

Assemble the Star Blocks

1. For accurate sewing lines, use a quilter's pencil to mark a diagonal line on the wrong sides of eight solid red 2" squares. (To prevent your fabric from stretching as you draw the lines, place 220-grit sandpaper under the pieces.)

2. Align a marked solid red 2" square with one end of a parchment print 2×3½" rectangle (see Diagram 1; note the placement of the marked diagonal line). Stitch on the marked line; trim the seam allowance to ¼". Press open the attached triangle. Sew a second marked solid red 2" square on the opposite end of the parchment print rectangle (See Diagram 1, again noting the placement of the marked line); Stitch, trim, and press as before to make a Flying Geese unit.

Diagram 1

3. Repeat Step 2 to make a total of four Flying Geese units (see Diagram 2). Each unit should measure 2×3½", including the seam allowances.

Diagram 2

4. Sew the Flying Geese units to opposite edges of a solid red 3½" square (see Diagram 3). Then add a parchment print 2" square to each end of the remaining two Flying Geese units. Join the units to the remaining edges of the red 3½" square to make a star block. Press all seam allowances away from the red square.

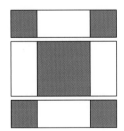

Diagram 3

5. Repeat steps 1 through 4 to make a total of 16 star blocks. Each pieced block should measure 6½" square, including the seam allowances.

Assemble the Puss in the Corner Blocks

1. Referring to Diagram 4 for placement, lay out one solid green 3½" square, four solid green 2" squares, and four parchment print 2×3½" rectangles in three horizontal rows.

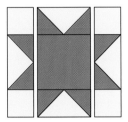

Diagram 4

2. Sew together the pieces in each row. Press the seam allowances toward the green squares. Then join the rows to make a Puss in the Corner block.

3. Repeat steps 1 and 2 to make a total of nine Puss in the Corner blocks. Each pieced block should measure 6½" square, including the seam allowances.

Appliqué the Heart Blocks

Referring to the photograph on *page 57* for placement, appliqué a solid red heart diagonally onto a parchment print 5½" square. Repeat to make a total of four appliquéd heart blocks.

Assemble the Quilt Center

1. Referring to the Quilt Assembly Diagram for placement, lay out the Puss in the Corner, star blocks, and parchment print side triangles in diagonal rows (the corner triangles will be added later).

2. Sew together the pieces in each row. Press the seam allowances toward the Puss in the Corner blocks. Then sew together the rows. Press the seam allowances in one direction. Add the parchment print corner triangles to complete the quilt center.

Add the Borders

1. Sew the solid green 1×34½" inner border strips to opposite edges of the quilt center. Then add the solid green 1×35½" inner border strips to the remaining edges of the quilt center. Press the seam allowances toward the solid green border strips.

Quilt Assembly Diagram

2. Sew the red-and-green plaid 5½×35½" outer border strips to opposite edges of the quilt center. Then add a heart block to each end of the remaining red-and-green plaid 5½×35½" outer border strips. Join the border strips to the remaining edges of the quilt center to complete the quilt top. Press the seam allowances toward the border strips.

Complete the Quilt

1. Layer the quilt top, batting, and backing according to the instructions in Quilting Basics, which begins on *page 91*.

2. Quilt as desired. Sylvia hand-quilted the stars, Puss in the Corner blocks, inner green border, and heart blocks in the ditch. Then she quilted around each heart, the corner triangles, and the border following the plaid. In the side triangles she quilted a small heart and leaves design.

3. Use the solid green 2½×42" strips to bind the quilt according to the instructions in Quilting Basics. Sew the Santa buttons on the green centers and the tree buttons on the red centers.

Color Option:
A soft pink-and-green rose print border fabric set the color scheme for this alternate version of the quilt.

Coordinating rose-color prints and mint green leaf prints contrast with the light print in the blocks and setting triangles.

pattern

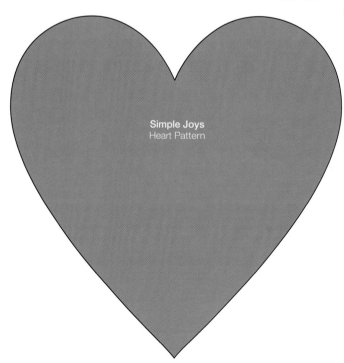

Simple Joys
Heart Pattern

don't stop
LEARNING

HERE'S A *cache* OF QUILT PROJECTS TO STRETCH YOUR SKILLS—INSPIRING IDEAS TO REPLICATE AND THEN RE-INVENT IN YOUR OWN FAVORITE FABRICS. LEARN TO APPLIQUÉ, ENJOY SPEEDY STRIP PIECING, OR LOSE ALL INHIBITION AND ENJOY A LITTLE CRAZY QUILTING!

Amish town SQUARES

Materials

Scraps of nine assorted solid jewel tones
for blocks
⅓ yard of solid black for setting squares
½ yard of solid rust for sashing and
binding
¼ yard of solid magenta for border
¾ yard of backing fabric
27" square of quilt batting

Finished quilt top: 20½" square
Finished block: 4" square

Quantities specified for 44/45"-wide,
100% cotton fabrics. All measurements
include a ¼" seam allowance. Sew
with right sides together unless
otherwise stated.

Photographs: Perry Struse;
Marcia Cameron

Cut the Fabrics

To make the best use of your fabrics, cut
the pieces in the order that follows.

*From each of nine assorted solid jewel
tones, cut:*
• 1—3" square for block center
From solid black, cut:
• 4—3" squares
• 18—2½" squares, cutting each in half
diagonally for a total of 36 corner
triangles
• 16—1¾" squares for sashing
From solid rust, cut:
• 3—2½×42" binding strips
• 24—1¾×4" sashing strips
From solid magenta, cut:
• 4—3×16" border strips

Assemble the Blocks

1. Sew solid black corner triangles to
opposite edges of a solid jewel-tone 3"
square (see Diagram 1). Press the seam
allowances toward the black triangles.

Diagram 1

2. Add the black corner triangles to the
remaining edges of the solid jewel-tone
squares to make a block (see Diagram 2).
Press the seam allowances away from the
solid jewel-tone square. The pieced block
should measure 4" square, including the
seam allowances.

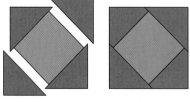

Diagram 2

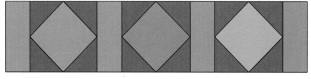

Diagram 3

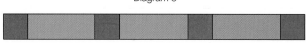

Diagram 4

3. Repeat steps 1 and 2 to make a total
of nine solid jewel-tone blocks.

Assemble the Rows

1. Sew together three pieced blocks
and four solid rust sashing strips in a
horizontal row, alternating them and
beginning and ending the row with a
sashing strip to make a block row (see
Diagram 3). Press the seam allowances in
one direction. The pieced block row
should measure 4×16", including the
seam allowances. Repeat to make a total
of three block rows.

2. Join four solid black 1¾" sashing
squares and three solid rust 1¾×4"
sashing strips in a horizontal row,
alternating them and beginning and
ending the row with a sashing square
to make a sashing row (see Diagram 4).
The pieced sashing row should
measure 1¾×16", including the seam
allowances. Repeat to make a total of
four sashing rows.

Assemble the Quilt Center

1. Referring to the photograph *opposite*
for placement, lay out the sashing and
block rows. Alternate the rows,
beginning and ending with a
sashing row.

THIS AGELESS *heirloom*, ROTARY CUT FOR EASY SPEED, REFLECTS THE DISCIPLINED USE OF COLOR PERFECTED BY THE AMISH.

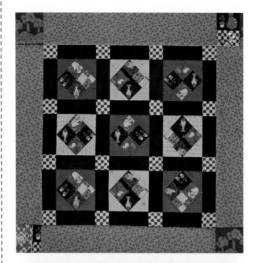

Color Options: The versatility of the block in "Amish Town Square" makes experimenting with colors fun. For example, *top*, cat-motif fabrics make a whimsical variation; solids create a brighter Amish coloration, and pinks, roses, plums, and blues offer a cheerful rendition.

color perfection by the Amish

2. Join the rows to make the quilt center. Press all seam allowances in one direction. The pieced quilt center should measure 16" square, including the seam allowances.

Add the Border

1. Sew solid magenta 3×16" border strips to opposite edges of the pieced quilt center. Press the seam allowances toward the border.

2. Join a solid black 3" square to each end of the remaining solid magenta 3×16" border strips to make pieced border strips. Press the seam allowances toward the solid magenta strips. Then sew the pieced border strips to the remaining edges of the quilt center to complete the quilt top. Press the seam allowances toward the border.

Complete the Quilt

1. Layer the quilt top, batting, and backing according to the instructions in Quilting Basics, which begins on *page 91.*

2. Quilt as desired. The wall hanging shown on *page 63* was machine-quilted with black thread. Pieced blocks were quilted in a diagonal grid, and the borders were quilted with a scroll design.

3. Use the solid rust 2$^{1}/_{2}$×42" strips to bind the quilt according to the instructions in Quilting Basics.

Cottontail

Folk art COMES ALIVE AS THIS FUNNY BUNNY HOPS THE STARS. TRIANGLES IN TWO SIZES AND EASY APPLIQUÉ MAKE THIS A GREAT WEEKEND PROJECT.

Materials

Scraps of assorted red, brown, black, and tan plaids for borders

¼ yard of off-white print for appliqué foundation

Scrap of brown stripe for bunny appliqué

Scraps of assorted red and brown prints and plaids for star appliqués

¼ yard of black plaid for binding

¾ yard of backing fabric

26×30" of quilt batting

Finished quilt top: 24×20"

Quantities specified for 44/45"–wide, 100% cotton fabrics. All measurements include a ¼" seam allowance. Sew with right sides together unless otherwise stated.

Design: Mary Tendall and Connie Tesene
Photograph: Perry Struse

Cut the Fabrics

To make the best use of your fabrics, cut the pieces in the order that follows. The patterns are *opposite*. To make templates of the patterns, follow the instructions in Quilting Basics, which begins on *page 91.*

From assorted red, brown, black, and tan plaid scraps, cut:
- 14—4⅞" squares, cutting each in half diagonally for a total of 28 large triangles
- 40—2⅞" squares, cutting each in half diagonally for a total of 80 small triangles

From off-white print, cut:
- 1—8½×12½" rectangle for appliqué foundation

From brown stripe, cut:
- 1 of Pattern A

From assorted red and brown print and plaid scraps, cut:
- 1 of Pattern B
- 2 of Pattern C

From black plaid, cut:
- 3—2×42" binding strips

Appliqué the Center Block

Referring to the photograph on *page 65* for placement, appliqué the brown strip bunny onto the off-white print foundation rectangle. Then appliqué the stars onto the foundation rectangle to make the center block.

Assemble the Units

1. Sew together two assorted red, brown, black, or tan plaid large triangles to make a large triangle-square (see Diagram 1). Press the seam allowances in one direction. The large triangle-square should measure 4½" square, including the seam allowances. Repeat to make a total of 14 large triangle-squares.

Diagram 2

Diagram 1

2. Sew together two assorted red, brown, black, and tan plaid small triangles to make a small triangle-square (see Diagram 2). Press the seam allowances in one direction. The small triangle-square should measure 2½" square, including the seam allowances. Repeat to make a total of 40 small triangle-squares.

Assemble the Quilt Top

1. Referring to the Quilt Assembly Diagram for placement, lay out the appliquéd center block, the large triangle-squares and the small triangle-squares in five horizontal rows.

2. Sew together the pieces in each row. Press the seam allowances in one direction. Then join the rows to complete the quilt top. Press the seam allowances in one direction.

Complete the Quilt

1. Layer the quilt top, batting, and backing according to the instructions in Quilting Basics, which begins on *page 91.*

2. Quilt as desired. Mary and Connie outlined the triangle-squares, the bunny, and the stars with hand quilting. They quilted large and small stars on the off-white print background to fill in space.

3. Use the black plaid 2×42" strips to bind the quilt according to the instructions in Quilting Basics.

Quilt Assembly Diagram

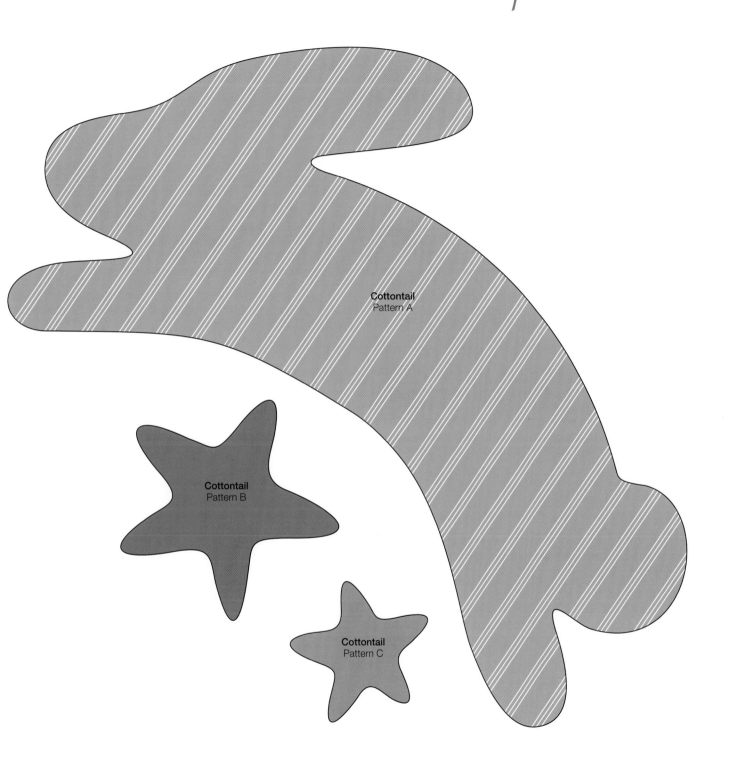

Cottontail
Pattern A

Cottontail
Pattern B

Cottontail
Pattern C

Spring STRIPES

Materials

2—⅓-yard pieces of assorted green plaids and stripes for setting squares and pieced blocks

10—⅓-yard pieces of assorted pink, blue, yellow, purple, and tan stripes and plaids for pieced blocks and outer border

1⅝ yards of green plaid for setting squares, pieced blocks, and binding

⅜ yard of pink stripe for pieced blocks and inner border

1½ yards of backing fabric

42×50" of quilt batting

Finished quilt top: 36×44"
Finished block: 4" square

Quantities specified for 44/45"-wide, 100% cotton fabrics. All measurements include a ¼" seam allowance. Sew with right sides together unless otherwise stated.

Design: Mabeth Oxenreider
Photograph: Steve Struse

Cut the Fabrics

To make the best use of your fabrics, cut the pieces in the order that follows.

From assorted green plaids and stripes, cut:
- 1—21" square, cutting it into enough 2½"-wide bias strips to total 170" for binding (For specific instructions on cutting bias strips, see Quilting Basics, which begins on *page 91.*)
- 5—22"-long strips in varying widths (Quiltmaker Mabeth Oxenreider used 1¼"- to 1¾"-wide strips.)
- 31—4½" squares

From assorted pink, blue, yellow, purple, and tan stripes and plaids, cut:
- 5—3½×42" strips for outer border
- 30—22"-long strips in varying widths

From pink stripe, cut:
- 2—1½×38½" inner border strips
- 2—1½×28½" inner border strips
- 5—22"-long strips in varying widths

FABRICS CUT INTO STRIPS, *sewn together*, AND THEN CUT TO SIZE: FOR QUICK QUILTS, STRIP PIECING IS THE BEST THING SINCE SLICED BREAD.

Assemble the Pieced Blocks

1. Sew together a random selection of 22"-long strips to make a strip set that is at least 4½" wide (see Diagram 1). Press the seam allowances in one direction. Repeat to make a total of eight strip sets. *Note:* You'll sew long fabric strips together more quickly and accurately by feeding the fabric through your sewing machine against a raised guide attachment or a piece of moleskin placed at the quarter-inch mark.

2. Cut each strip set into four 4½"-wide segments (see Diagram 2). Trim each 4½"-wide segment into a pieced block that is 4½" square, including the seam allowances (see Diagram 3). Repeat to make a total of 32 pieced blocks.

Assemble the Quilt Center

1. Referring to the photograph *opposite* for placement, lay out the 32 pieced blocks and the 31 green plaid and stripe 4½" squares in nine horizontal rows, alternating the squares.

2. Sew together the squares in each row. Press the seam allowances toward the green plaid or stripe squares. Then join the rows to make the quilt center. Press the seam allowances in one direction. The pieced quilt center should measure 28½×36½", including the seam allowances.

Add the Borders

1. Sew the pink stripe 1½×28½" inner border strips to the top and bottom edges of the pieced quilt center. Then join the pink stripe 1½×38½" inner border strips to the side edges. Press all seam allowances toward the inner border.

2. Cut and piece the five assorted pink, blue, yellow, purple, and tan stripe and plaid 3½×42" strips with diagonal seams to make the following:

- 2—3½×44½" outer border strips
- 2—3½×30½" outer border strips

3. Sew the short pieced outer border strips to the top and bottom edges of the pieced quilt center. Then join the long pieced outer border strips to the side edges to complete the quilt top. Press all seam allowances toward the outer border.

Complete the Quilt

1. Layer the quilt top, batting, and backing according to the instructions in Quilting Basics, which begins on *page 91.*

2. Quilt as desired. Mabeth machine-quilted a simple flower design in each green 4" square, connecting the flowers with a meandering allover pattern.

3. Use the green plaid 2½"-wide bias strips to bind the quilt according to the instructions in Quilting Basics.

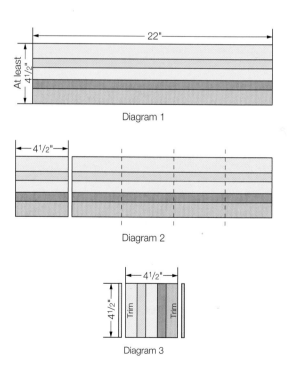

Diagram 1

Diagram 2

Diagram 3

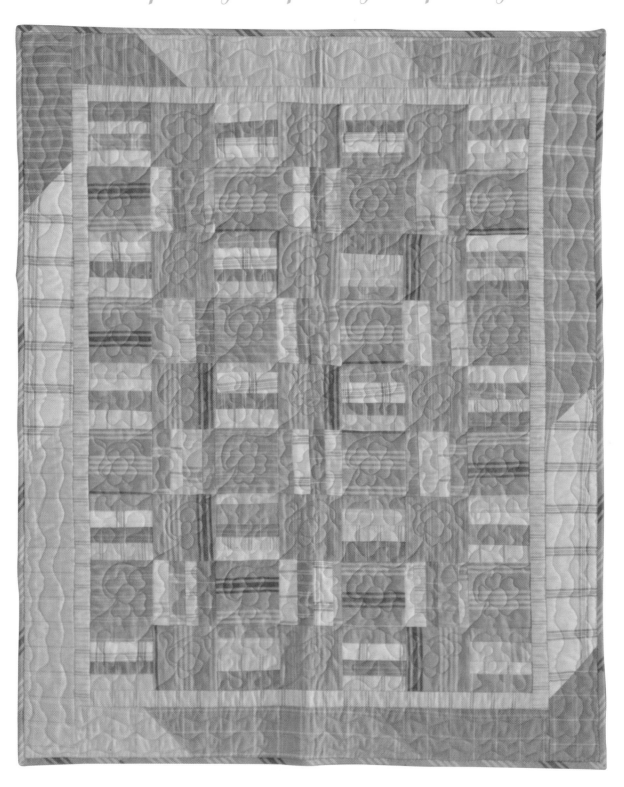

CRAZY for you

THIS *free-spirited* QUILT GOES TOGETHER QUICKLY BECAUSE IT'S MADE OF ONE CRAZY BLOCK REPEATED IN A WHIRLWIND OF COLOR.

Materials

2¾ yards of muslin for block foundations
8—⅓-yard pieces of assorted black prints
    for blocks, outer border, and binding
13—⅓-yard pieces of assorted light prints
    for blocks
6—⅓-yard pieces of assorted medium
    prints for blocks
⅓ yard of red print for blocks and
    inner border
3⅛ yards of backing fabric
3⅛ yards of flannel for quilt batting
Machine-embroidery thread in
    assorted colors

Finished quilt top: 50×70"
Finished block: 10" square

Quantities specified for 44/45"-wide, 100% cotton fabrics. All measurements include a ¼" seam allowance. Sew with right sides together unless otherwise stated.

Design: Mabeth Oxenreider
Photograph: Perry Struse

Designer Notes

The first step in making a crazy quilt? "Make sure you have lots of different fabric," designer Mabeth Oxenreider says. "The more you have, the more random and interesting it can be. You cannot have too much fabric."

For this quilt, Mabeth started with more than 20 assorted prints in white, pink, blue, yellow, red, and black. Her selection included checks, florals, and novelty prints. "I didn't measure anything; I just whacked out five-sided shapes for the centers." She cut strips for the other pieces and alternated fabrics at random as she pieced her way around each block.

"After each round was added, I'd do my decorative stitching," Mabeth explains. Although it took a little more time to complete the blocks this way, she was able to hide ends of each row of decorative stitches within the seams.

Her stitching was also random. "You have all those stitches on that sewing machine; use them," she says. "Quite honestly, it's the first time I used some of the stitches on mine."

Cut the Fabrics

To make the best use of your fabrics, cut the pieces in the order that follows.

From muslin, cut:
• 24—12" squares for foundations
   (these foundations will be trimmed
   after the blocks are pieced)
From assorted black prints, cut:
• 6—2½×42" binding strips
• 12—4½×23" strips for outer border
From red print, cut:
• 6—1½×42" strips for inner border

Assemble and Embellish the Blocks

The instructions that follow call for assembling all of the blocks, then embellishing them.

1. From an assorted light or medium print, cut a block center piece with five sides. (The center pieces in the quilt shown *opposite* measure approximately 3½×4" at their widest points.) Pin the center piece onto a muslin 12" square block foundation at the approximate center.

2. Cut a variety of light, medium, and black pieces in assorted shapes and sizes. The pieces must be cut with straight, not curved, edges.

3. Place a second print piece over the center piece, aligning a pair of edges. Sew together along the aligned edges (see Diagram 1).

Diagram 1

4. Press the top piece open (see Diagram 2 on *page 74*). Being careful not to cut through the muslin foundation, use a scissors to trim the ends of the second piece so that they're even with the center piece.

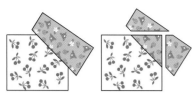

Diagram 2

5. Position a third print piece on the pieced unit, aligning a pair of edges. Sew together along the aligned edges. Press open and trim as before.

6. Repeat the process until the entire muslin block foundation is covered, trimming any fabric pieces that extend past the foundation edges, to make a crazy quilt block.

7. Repeat steps 1 through 6 to make a total of 24 blocks.

8. Using decorative machine stitches and contrasting machine-embroidery thread, embellish the seam lines of each crazy quilt block as desired.

9. Trim the completed embellished crazy quilt blocks to 10½" square, keeping the first print piece as close to the center of each block as possible.

Assemble the Quilt Center

1. Referring to the photograph *above right* for placement, lay out the blocks in six horizontal rows.

2. Sew together the blocks in each row. Press the seam allowances in one direction, alternating the direction with each row. Then join the rows to make the quilt center. Press the seam allowances in one direction. The pieced quilt center should measure 40½×60½", including the seam allowances.

Add the Borders

1. Cut and piece the red print 1½×42" strips to make the following:
• 2—1½×60½" inner border strips
• 2—1½×42½" inner border strips

2. Sew the long red print inner border strips to the side edges of the pieced quilt center. Then join the short red print inner border strips to the top and bottom edges of the quilt center. Press all seam allowances toward the inner border.

3. Cut and piece the assorted black print 4½×23" strips with diagonal seams to make the following:
• 2—4½×62½" outer border strips
• 2—4½×50½" outer border strips

4. Add the long black print outer border strips to the side edges of the pieced quilt center. Then join the short black print outer border strips to the top and bottom edges of the quilt center to complete the quilt top. Press all seam allowances toward the outer border.

Complete the Quilt

1. Layer the quilt top, flannel, and backing according to the instructions in Quilting Basics, which begins on *page 91.*

2. Quilt as desired. Because these blocks are heavily embellished with decorative stitching, designer Mabeth Oxenreider chose to use flannel as the batting. This allowed her to space her quilting stitches farther apart than is traditional, stitching only in the ditch between the blocks and on the borders.

3. Use the black print 2½×42" strips to bind the quilt according to the instructions in Quilting Basics.

The WARMTH OF HOME

Greet guests TO YOUR HOME WITH THIS TRADITIONAL WELCOME MOTIF. THE LARGE SHAPES ARE PERFECT FOR PERFECTING YOUR APPLIQUÉ SKILLS.

Materials

1—18×22" piece (fat quarter) of dark red mottled flannel for appliqué foundation

1—9×22" piece (fat eighth) of solid dark gold flannel for pineapple appliqué

Scrap of green plaid flannel for leaf appliqués

Scrap of purple print for base appliqués

1—18×22" piece (fat quarter) of tan mottled flannel for border

4—2½" squares of tan plaid flannel for border

26×28" of cotton quilt batting

Embroidery floss: brick red and antique gold

Double-faced, wax-free tracing paper: white (Designer Miriam Gourley used a product from Prym-Dritz.)

Finished quilt top (unframed): 20×21½"

Quantities specified for 44/45"-wide, 100% cotton fabrics. All measurements include a ¼" seam allowance. Sew with right sides together unless otherwise stated.

Design: Miriam Gourley
Photograph: Scott Little

Cut the Fabrics

To make the best use of your fabrics, cut the pieces in the order that follows. The patterns are *opposite*. To make templates of the patterns, follow the instructions in Quilting Basics, which begins on *page 91*.

From dark red mottled flannel, cut:
- 1—16½×18" rectangle for appliqué foundation

From solid dark gold flannel, cut:
- 1 of Pattern A

From green plaid flannel scrap, cut:
- 1 *each* of patterns B, C, C reversed, D, and D reversed

From purple print scrap, cut:
- 1 *each* of patterns E and E reversed

From tan mottled flannel, cut:
- 2—2½×16½" border strips
- 2—2½×18" border strips

Assemble the Quilt Top

1. Aligning long raw edges, sew a tan mottled 2½×16½" border strip to each short edge of the dark red mottled 16½×18" appliqué foundation. Press the seam allowances toward the tan border.

2. Sew a tan plaid 2½" square to each end of the tan mottled 2½×18" border strips to make two border units. Press the seam allowances toward the tan mottled strips.

3. Sew a border unit to each remaining edge of the dark red mottled appliqué foundation to make the quilt center. Press the seam allowance toward the tan border.

Add the Appliqués

1. Referring to the Assembly Diagram for placement, lay out the appliqué shapes on the quilt top. The base of the pineapple should be approximately 2¾" from the border seam. When you are pleased with the arrangement, baste the shapes in place.

2. Using threads in colors that match the appliqué shapes, appliqué the pieces to the quilt top.

Assembly Diagram

Embroider the Quilt Top

1. Using antique gold embroidery floss, Miriam embroidered a series of small upright cross-stitches and French knots across the appliquéd pineapple to give it texture (see Pineapple Embroidery Diagram).

Pineapple Embroidery Diagram

Use two strands of embroidery floss for the upright cross-stitch. To make an upright cross-stitch (see diagram *below*), bring your needle up at A, go down at B. Bring your needle up at C, cross over the first stitch, and push the needle down at D to make a cross.

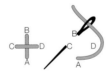

Upright Cross-Stitch

To make a French knot, pull your needle and one strand of floss through at A, the point where the knot is desired (see diagram *below*). Wrap the floss around the needle two times without twisting it. Insert the tip of the needle into the fabric at B, ¹⁄₁₆" away from A. Gently push the wraps down the needle to meet the fabric. Pull the needle and trailing floss through the fabric slowly and smoothly.

French Knot

2. Using the double-faced, wax-free tracing paper, trace the lettering. Be sure it is centered 2" above the top point of the center pineapple leaf and 2" below the border seam.

3. Using two strands of antique gold floss, stem-stitch the lettering.

To stem-stitch, pull your needle up at A (see diagram *below*), then insert the needle back into the fabric at B, about ¼" away from A. Holding the floss out of the way, bring the needle back up at C and pull the floss through so it lies flat against the fabric. The distances between points A, B, and C should be equal. Pull with equal tautness after each stitch. Continue in the same manner, holding the floss out of the way on the same side every time.

Stem Stitch

Complete the Quilt

1. Layer the appliquéd quilt top and the batting; baste in place.

2. Using six strands of brick red embroidery floss, make running stitches around the outside edge of the dark red mottled rectangle and around the appliquéd pieces.

To make running stitches, pull your needle up at A and push it down at B (see diagram *below*). Continue stitching to the left, taking evenly spaced stitches.

Running Stitch

3. Have the finished piece professionally stretched and framed, or frame it yourself.

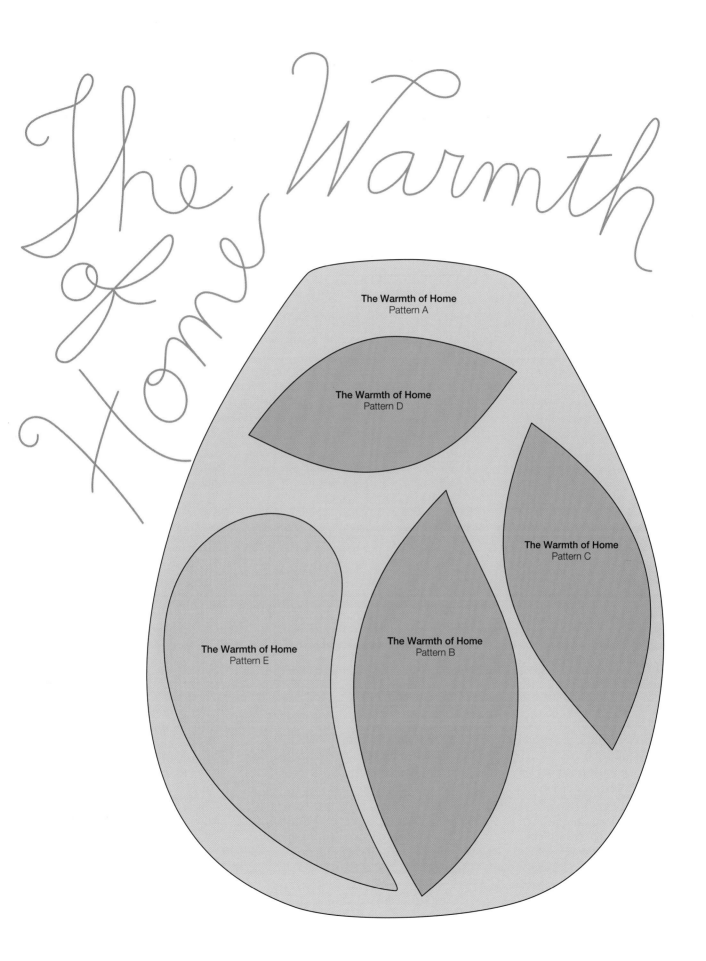

The Warmth of Home
Pattern A

The Warmth of Home
Pattern D

The Warmth of Home
Pattern C

The Warmth of Home
Pattern E

The Warmth of Home
Pattern B

Materials

9—¼-yard pieces of assorted dark prints for blocks, pieced border, corner blocks, and binding

9—¼-yard pieces of assorted gold, orange, and red prints for blocks and pieced border

9—⅓-yard pieces of assorted tan prints for blocks, inner border, and corner blocks

⅛ yard of dark green print for corner blocks

⅛ yard of tan print for corner blocks

1—3×12" piece of gold print for corner blocks

3¼ yards of backing fabric

58" square of quilt batting

Finished quilt top: 52" square
Finished block: 12" square

Quantities specified for 44/45"-wide, 100% cotton fabrics. All measurements include a ¼" seam allowance. Sew with right sides together unless otherwise stated.

Design: Jill Reber
Photographs: Scott Little;
    Marcia Cameron

Cut the Fabrics

To make the best use of your fabrics, cut the pieces in the order that follows.

From each of 9 assorted dark prints, cut:
• 2—5¼" squares, cutting each diagonally twice in an X for a total of 8 large triangles
• 1—2½×26" strip for binding
• 4—2½×6½" rectangles
• 4—2⅞" squares, cutting each in half diagonally for a total of 8 small triangles

From each of 9 assorted gold, orange, and red prints, cut:
• 1—4½" square
• 5—2½×6½" rectangles
• 4—2½" squares

From remaining assorted gold, orange, and red prints, cut:
• 4—2½×4½" rectangles

From each of 9 assorted tan prints, cut:
• 2—5¼" squares, cutting each diagonally twice in an X for a total of 8 large triangles
• 4—2⅞" squares, cutting each in half diagonally for a total of 8 small triangles
• 4—2½" squares

From remaining assorted tan prints, cut:
• 12—2½×6½" rectangles
• 16—2½×5½" rectangles

From dark green print, cut:
• 4—2⅞" squares, cutting each in half diagonally for a total of 8 small triangles
• 3—2½×6½" rectangles for pieced border

From tan print, cut:
• 4—2⅞" squares, cutting each in half diagonally for a total of 8 small triangles
• 4—2½" squares

From gold print, cut:
• 4—2½" squares

Assemble the Star Blocks

1. For one star block you'll need eight small triangles and eight large triangles from the same dark print, one 4½" square and four 2½" squares from the same gold, orange, or red print, and four 2½" squares, eight small triangles, and eight large triangles from the same tan print.

2. Sew together a dark print small triangle and a tan print small triangle to make a triangle-square (see Diagram 1).

Press the seam allowance toward the dark print triangle. The pieced triangle-square should measure 2½" square, including the seam allowances. Repeat to make a total of eight triangle-squares.

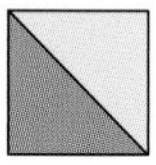

Diagram 1

3. Referring to Diagram 2 for placement, sew a triangle-square to a tan print 2½" square to make a subunit. Press the seam allowance toward the tan print square. Sew a triangle-square to a gold, orange, or red print 2½" square to make a second subunit. Press the seam allowance toward the gold, orange, or red print square. Sew the two subunits together to make a corner unit; press. The pieced corner unit should measure 4½" square, including the seam allowances. Repeat to make a total of four corner units.

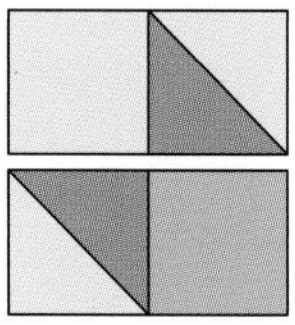

Diagram 2

4. Referring to Diagram 3, lay out two dark print large triangles and two tan print large triangles in pairs. Sew together the triangles in each pair. Press the seam allowances toward the dark print triangles. Then join the triangle pairs to make a triangle unit. Press the seam allowance in one direction. The pieced

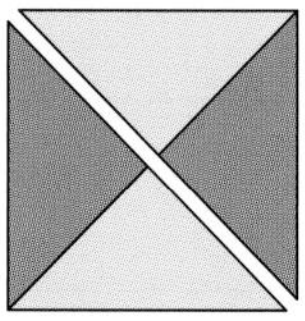

Diagram 3

STAR

BUILD YOUR *stash of fabric* WHILE MAKING THIS CHARMING SCRAPPY QUILT. OR PULL FROM YOUR EXISTING COLLECTION AND FIND A HOME FOR THOSE BITS AND PIECES.

triangle unit should measure 4½" square, including the seam allowances. Repeat to make a total of four triangle units.

5. Referring to Diagram 4, lay out the pieced corner and triangle units and the gold, orange, or red print 4½" square in three horizontal rows. Sew together the pieces in each row. Press the seam allowances in alternating directions. Then join the rows to make a star block. Press the seam allowances in one direction. The pieced star block should measure 12½" square, including the seam allowances.

Diagram 4

6. Repeat steps 1 through 5 to make a total of nine star blocks.

Assemble the Quilt Center

1. Referring to the photograph *opposite* for placement, lay out the nine pieced star blocks in three horizontal rows.

2. Sew together the blocks in each row. Press the seam allowances in one direction, alternating the direction with each row. Then join the rows to complete the quilt center. Press the seam allowances in one direction. The pieced quilt center should measure 36½" square, including the seam allowances.

Assemble and Add the Borders

1. Aligning short edges, join six assorted tan print 2½×6½" rectangles to make the top pieced inner border strip. Press the seam allowances in one direction. The pieced border strip should measure 2½×36½", including the seam allowances. Repeat to make the bottom pieced inner border strip. Add the border strips to the top and bottom edges of the pieced quilt center. Press the seam allowances toward the quilt center.

2. Aligning short edges, sew together eight assorted tan print 2½×5½" rectangles to make a pieced side border strip. Press the seam allowances in one direction. The pieced side border strip should measure 2½×40½", including seam allowances. Repeat to make a second side pieced inner border strip. Add the border strips to the side edges of the pieced quilt center. Press the seam allowances toward the quilt center.

3. Aligning long edges, sew together 20 assorted dark print, dark green print, and gold, orange, and red print 2½×6½" rectangles to make a pieced outer border strip. Press the seam allowances in one direction. The pieced outer border strip should measure 6½×40½", including seam allowances. Repeat to make a total of four pieced outer border strips. Add an outer border strip to the top and bottom edges of the pieced quilt center. Press the seam allowances toward the quilt center.

4. Referring to Assemble the Star Blocks, steps 2 and 3, use the dark green print A

triangles, the tan print A triangles, the tan print 2½" squares, and the gold print 2½" squares to make a total of four corner units.

5. Sew a gold, orange, or red print 2½×4½" rectangle and a dark print 2½×6½" rectangle to adjacent edges of each corner unit (see Diagram 5) to make four border corner blocks. Press the seam allowances toward the rectangles. The pieced corner border blocks should measure 6½" square, including the seam allowances.

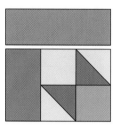

Diagram 5

6. Sew a border corner block to each end of the remaining pieced outer border strips. Press the seam allowances toward the pieced border strips. Add the border strips to the side edges of the pieced quilt center to complete the quilt top. Press the seam allowances toward the pieced border strips.

Complete the Quilt

1. Layer the quilt top, batting, and backing according to the instructions in Quilting Basics, which begins on *page 91*. Quilt as desired.

2. Use the dark print 2½×26" strips to bind the quilt according to the instructions in Quilting Basics.

house PARTY

Materials

1⅝ yards of solid black for appliqué foundations and outer border

⅝ yard of purple print for inner border and binding

⅓ yard of green print for checkerboard sashing, corner blocks, and star foundations

⅓ yard of multicolor print for checkerboard sashing, corner blocks, and star appliqués

1½ yards total of assorted bright prints, plaids, solids, and stripes for house foundations and roof, wall, door, window, and chimney appliqués

2¾ yards of backing fabric

49×71" of quilt batting

Freezer paper

Variegated thread for machine quilting

5 small buttons for doorknobs

Finished quilt top: 44×52"

Quantities specified for 44/45"-wide, 100% cotton fabrics. All measurements include a ¼" seam allowance. Sew with right sides together unless otherwise stated.

Design: Jenni Paige
Photograph: Steve Struse

Designer Notes

Striving to make quilting enjoyable for quilters of all levels, Idaho designer Jenni Paige focuses on quilting methods that often break traditional quilting "rules." Here she allowed her appliqué pieces to fray and wound up with a fun and funky wall hanging. To replicate her efforts, Jenni suggests following these tips:

Each house foundation piece is one piece of fabric upon which the house walls, roof, door, windows and chimney are built. Select fabrics for the house foundations that coordinate with the wall and roof fabrics as the foundations are slightly visible along the house's frayed edges.

"Use your collection of 'oops' fabrics for the house foundations," Jenni says. "Because the foundations won't show, except slightly around the edges, this is a great place to use your ugly prints or flawed fabrics."

For a more frayed look, choose loosely woven fabrics; tightly woven fabrics will mean less fraying.

Set your sewing machine's stitch length to 12 to 15 stitches per inch. This will ensure nothing comes apart during machine washing.

Cut the Fabrics

To make the best use of your fabrics, cut the pieces in the order that follows. The patterns are on *pages 86–90.*

To use freezer paper for cutting the appliqué shapes, as was done in this project, complete the following steps. Each appliqué shape is cut to its finished size; no seam allowances need to be added.

1. Lay the freezer paper, shiny side down, over the patterns. Use a pencil to trace each pattern the number of times indicated, leaving a ¼" space between tracings. Cut out each piece on the drawn lines.

2. Using a hot, dry iron, press the freezer-paper shapes, shiny side down, onto the front of the designated fabrics; let cool. Cut out the fabric shapes on the drawn lines. Peel off the freezer paper.

From solid black, cut:
- 3—3½×42" strips for outer border
- 3—12½×36½" strips for appliqué foundations
- 2—3½×36½" outer border strips

From purple print, cut:
- 5—2½×42" binding strips
- 3—1½×42" strips for inner border
- 2—1½×36½" inner border strips

From green print, cut:
- 3—2½×42" strips

From multicolor print, cut:
- 3—2½×42" strips

From assorted bright prints, plaids, solids and stripes, cut:
- 3 *each* of entire Pattern 1 house foundation, roof, and wall
- 3 *each* of entire Pattern 2 house foundation, roof, and wall
- 3 *each* of entire Pattern 3 house foundation, roof, and wall
- 3 *each* of entire Pattern 4 house foundation, roof, and wall
- 4 *each* of patterns 5 and 9
- 8 *each* of patterns 6, 7, and 8
- 7 of Pattern 10

From green print, cut:
- 12 of Pattern 11

From multicolor print, cut:
- 12 of Pattern 11

Frayed A BIT ABOUT THE EDGES, THESE COZY APPLIQUÉ COTTAGES ISSUE AN IRRESISTIBLE INVITATION TO COZY UP WITH HOT SPICED CIDER.

party....party....party

Appliqué the Houses

1. Referring to the photograph *above* for placement, arrange the 12 house foundation appliqués on the three solid black 12½×36½" appliqué foundations. Position the 12 wall and 12 roof appliqués on the corresponding house foundations, layering as needed, and pin in place. Position the seven chimney appliqués in place and pin.

2. Machine-appliqué the pieces in place, stitching ¼" from the raw edges to complete the appliquéd house strips. (The remaining appliqués will be added once the quilt is completed.)

Assemble the Quilt Center

1. Aligning long edges, sew together one green print 2½×42" strip and one multicolor print 2½×42" strip to make a strip set (see Diagram 1). Press the seam allowance toward the green print strip. Repeat to make a total of three strip sets.

2. Cut the strip sets into 2½"-wide segments for a total of 44.

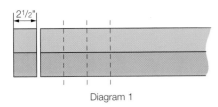

Diagram 1

3. Referring to Diagram 2 for placement, sew together eighteen 2½"-wide segments to make a checkerboard sashing strip. Press the seam allowances in one direction. The pieced checkerboard sashing strip should measure 4½×36½", including the seam allowances. Repeat to make a second checkerboard sashing strip. Set aside the remaining eight 2½"-wide segments for the border.

4. Referring to the photograph *opposite* for placement, lay out the three appliquéd house strips and the two checkerboard sashing strips in five horizontal rows. Join the rows to make the quilt center. Press the seam allowances in one direction, alternating the direction with each row.

Add the Borders

1. Join two remaining 2½"-wide segments to make a Four-Patch block (see Diagram 3). Press the seam allowance in one direction. The pieced Four-Patch block should measure 4½" square, including the seam allowances. Repeat to make a total of four Four-Patch blocks.

Diagram 3

2. Cut and piece the purple print 1½×42" strips to make the following:
- 2—1½×44½" inner border strips

3. Cut and piece the solid black 3½×42" strips to make the following:
- 2—3½×44½" outer border strips

4. Align the long edges of a purple print inner border strip and a solid black outer border strip; join to make a side border unit. Press the seam allowance toward the solid black strip. Repeat to make a second side border unit. Sew the side border units to the side edges of the pieced quilt center. Press the seam allowances toward the border.

5. Aligning the long edges of a purple print 1½×36½" strip and a solid black 3½×36½" strip, sew together to make the top border unit. Press the seam allowance toward the solid black strip. Repeat to make the bottom border unit.

6. Referring to the photograph *opposite* for placement, sew a Four-Patch block to each end of the top and bottom border units. Press the seam allowances toward the Four-Patch blocks. Join the pieced border units to the top and bottom edges of the pieced quilt center to complete the quilt top. Press the seam allowances toward the border.

Complete the Quilt

1. Layer the quilt top, batting, and backing according to the instructions in Quilting Basics, which begins on *page 91.*

2. Quilt as desired. Jenni machine-quilted her project in a meandering pattern with scattered star shapes.

3. Referring to the photograph *opposite* for placement, appliqué patterns 5, 6, 7, 8, 9, and 11 to the quilt using ¼" seam allowances. Machine-stitch panes in each window.

4. Use the purple print 2½×42" strips to bind the quilt according to the instructions in Quilting Basics.

5. After binding, wash the quilt in warm, soapy water and machine-dry to fray the edges. Trim any loose threads. Press, if needed.

6. Attach buttons to doors for knobs.

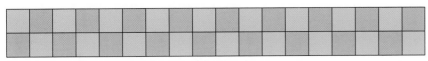

Diagram 2

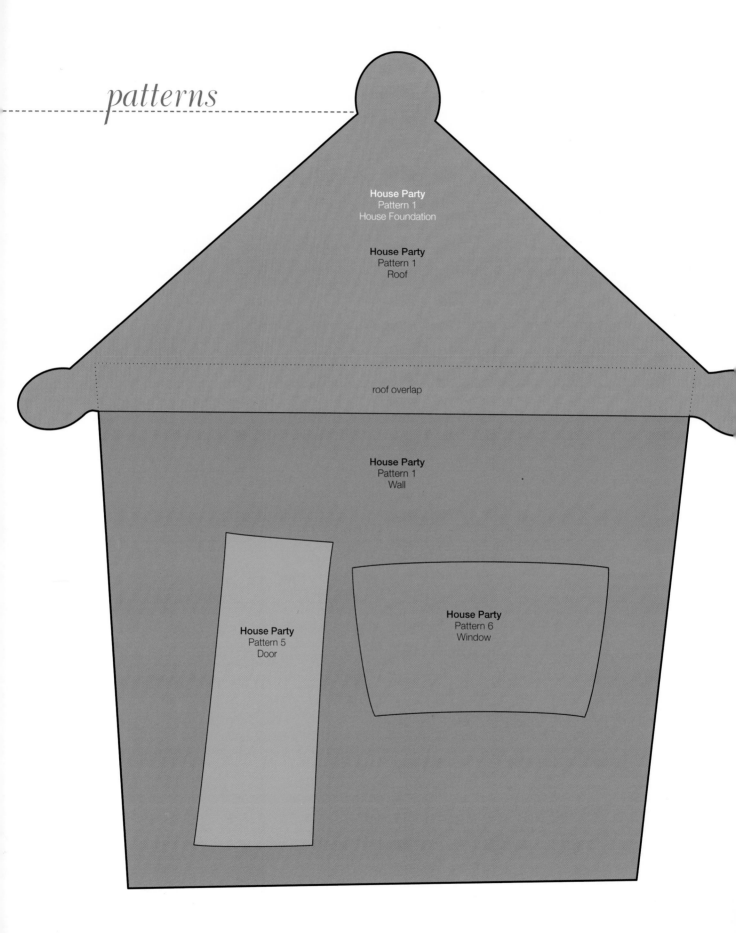

House Party
Pattern 1
House Foundation

House Party
Pattern 1
Roof

roof overlap

House Party
Pattern 1
Wall

House Party
Pattern 5
Door

House Party
Pattern 6
Window

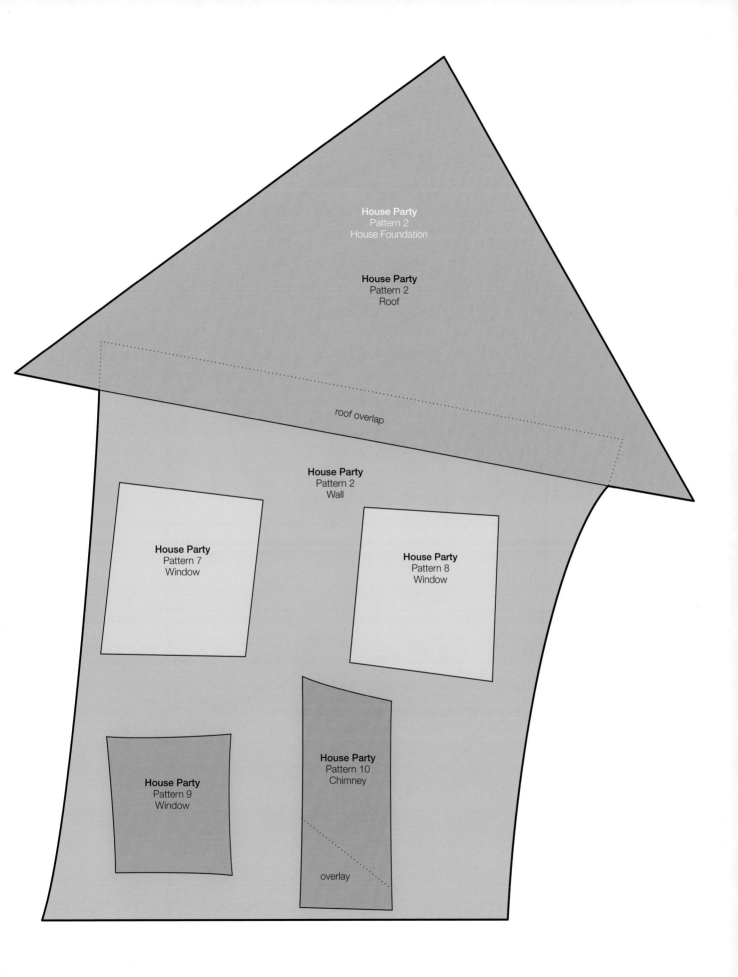

House Party
Pattern 2
House Foundation

House Party
Pattern 2
Roof

roof overlap

House Party
Pattern 2
Wall

House Party
Pattern 7
Window

House Party
Pattern 8
Window

House Party
Pattern 9
Window

House Party
Pattern 10
Chimney

overlay

patterns

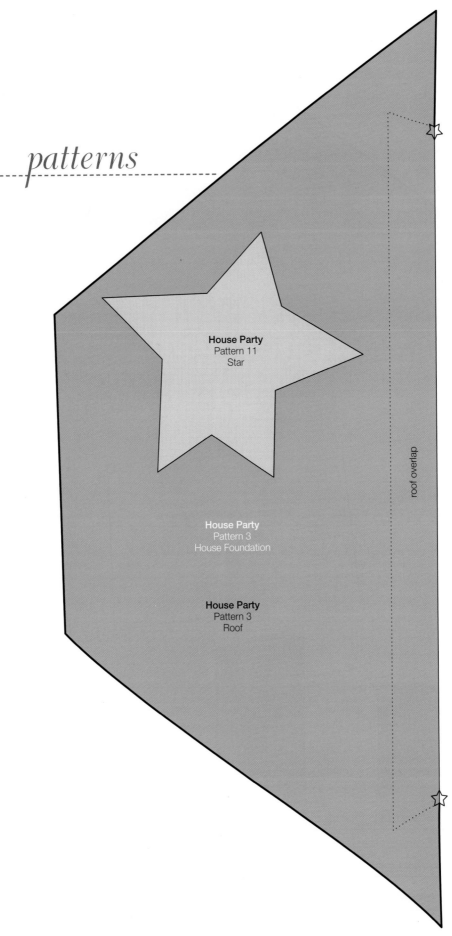

House Party
Pattern 11
Star

House Party
Pattern 3
House Foundation

House Party
Pattern 3
Roof

roof overlap

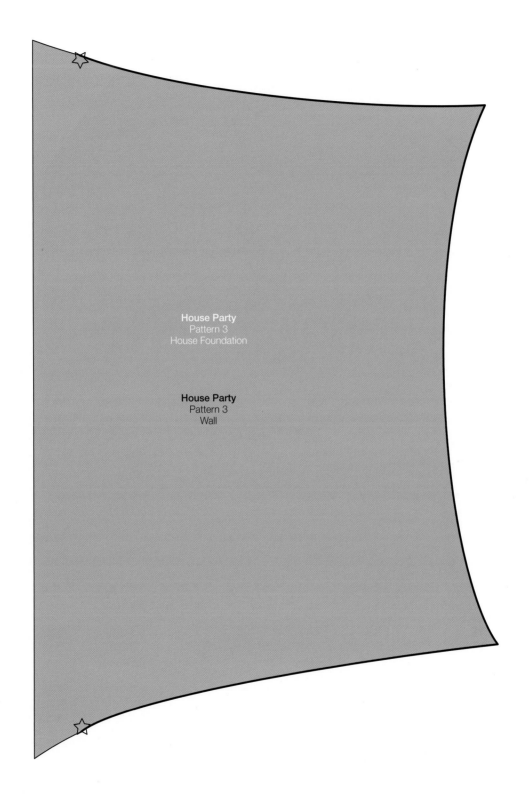

House Party
Pattern 3
House Foundation

House Party
Pattern 3
Wall

pattern

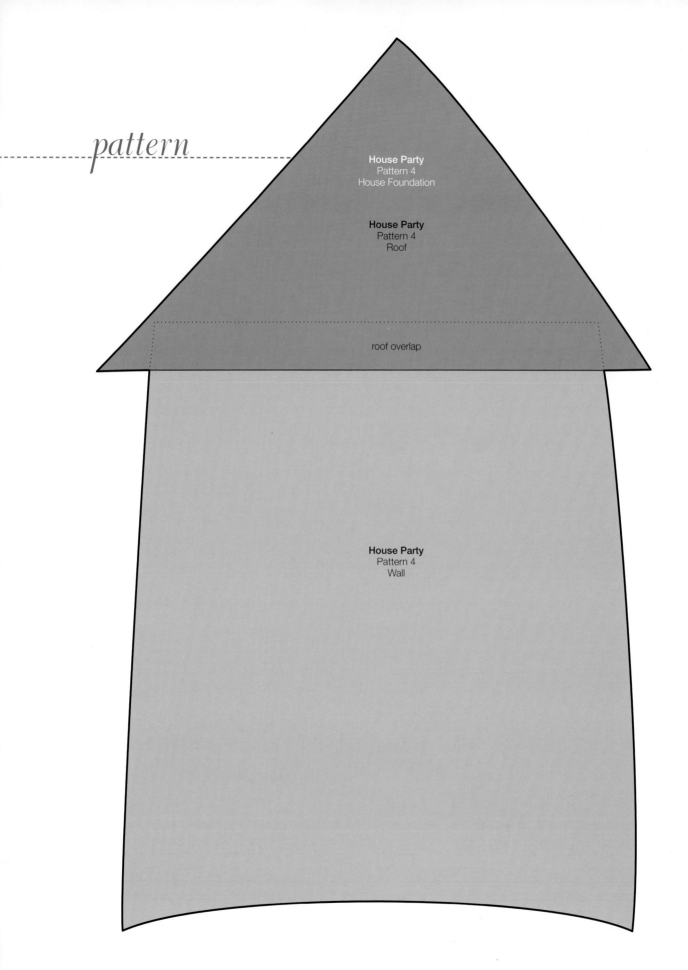

House Party
Pattern 4
House Foundation

House Party
Pattern 4
Roof

roof overlap

House Party
Pattern 4
Wall

QUILTING BASICS

GETTING STARTED

Cutting

Acrylic ruler: For making perfectly straight cuts with a rotary cutter, choose a ruler of thick, clear plastic. Many sizes are available. A 6×24" ruler marked in ¼" increments with 30°, 45°, and 60° angles is a good first purchase.

Rotary-cutting mat: A rotary cutter should always be used with a mat designed specifically for it. In addition to protecting the table, the mat helps keep the fabric from shifting while you cut. Often these mats are described as self-healing, meaning the blade does not leave slash marks or grooves in the surface, even after repeated usage. While many shapes and styles are available, a 16×23" mat marked with a 1" grid, with hash marks at ⅛" increments and 45° and 60° angles is a good choice.

Rotary cutter: The round blade of a rotary cutter will cut up to six layers of fabric at once. Because the blade is so sharp, be sure to purchase one with a safety guard, and keep the guard over the blade when you're not cutting. The blade can be removed from the handle and replaced when it gets dull. Commonly available in three sizes, a good first blade is a 45mm.

Scissors: You'll need one pair for fabric and another for paper and plastic.

Pencils and other marking tools: Marks made with special quilt markers are easy to remove after sewing.

Template plastic: This slightly frosted plastic comes in sheets about 1⁄16" thick.

Piecing

Iron and ironing board

Sewing thread: Use 100-percent-cotton thread.

Sewing machine: Any machine in good working order with well-adjusted tension will produce pucker-free patchwork seams.

Applique

Fusible web: Instead of the traditional method, secure cutout shapes to the background of an appliqué block with this iron-on adhesive.

Hand-sewing needles: For hand appliqué, most quilters like fine quilting needles.

Hand Quilting

Frame or hoop: You'll get smaller, more even stitches if you stretch your quilt as you stitch. A frame supports the quilt's weight, ensures even tension, and frees both your hands for stitching. However, once set up, it cannot be disassembled until the quilting is complete. Quilting hoops are more portable and less expensive.

Quilting needles: A "between" or quilting needle is short with a small eye. Common sizes are 8, 9, and 10; size 8 is best for beginners.

Quilting thread: Quilting thread is stronger than sewing thread.

Thimble: This finger cover relieves the pressure required to push a needle through several layers of fabric and batting.

Machine Quilting

Darning foot: You may find this tool, also called a hopper foot, in your sewing machine's accessory kit. If not, have the model and brand of your machine available when you go to purchase one. It is used for free-motion stitching.

Safety pins: They hold the layers together during quilting.

Table: Use a large work surface that's level with your machine bed.

Thread: Use 100-percent-cotton quilting thread, cotton-wrapped polyester quilting thread, or very fine nylon monofilament thread.

Walking foot: This sewing-machine accessory helps you keep long, straight quilting lines smooth and pucker-free.

Choose Your Fabrics

It is no surprise that most quilters prefer 100-percent-cotton fabrics for quiltmaking. Cotton fabric minimizes seam distortion, presses crisply, and is easy to quilt. Most patterns, including those in this book, specify quantities for 44/45"-wide fabrics unless otherwise noted. Our projects call for a little extra yardage in length to allow for minor errors and slight shrinkage.

Prepare Your Fabrics

There are conflicting opinions about the need to prewash fabric. The debate is a modern one because most antique quilts were made with unwashed fabric. However, the dyes and sizing used today are unlike those used a century ago.

Prewashing fabric offers quilters certainty as its main advantage. Today's fabrics resist bleeding and shrinkage, but some of both can occur in some fabrics—an unpleasant prospect once you've assembled the quilt. Some quilters find prewashed fabric easier to quilt. If you choose to prewash your fabric, press it well before cutting.

Other quilters prefer the crispness of unwashed fabric for machine piecing. And, if you use fabrics with the same fiber content throughout the quilt, then any shrinkage that occurs in its first washing should be uniform. Some quilters find this small amount of shrinkage desirable, since it gives the quilt a slightly puckered, antique look.

We recommend you prewash a scrap of each fabric to test it for shrinkage and bleeding. If you choose to prewash a fabric, unfold it to a single layer. Wash it in warm water to allow the fabric to shrink and/or bleed. If the fabric bleeds, rinse it until the water runs clear. Don't use any fabric in your quilt if it hasn't stopped bleeding. Hang fabric to dry, or tumble it in the dryer until slightly damp.

Press for Success

In quilting, almost every seam needs to be pressed before the piece is sewn to another, so keep your iron and ironing board near your sewing area. It's important to remember to press with an up and down motion. Moving the iron around on the fabric can distort seams, especially those sewn on the bias.

Project instructions in this book generally tell you in what direction to press each seam. When in doubt, press both seam allowances toward the darker fabric. When joining rows of blocks, alternate the direction the seam allowances are pressed to ensure flat corners.

CUTTING BIAS STRIPS

Strips for curved appliqué pattern pieces, such as meandering vines, and for binding curved edges should be cut on the bias (diagonally across the grain of a woven fabric), which runs at a 45° angle to the selvage and has the most give or stretch.

To cut bias strips, begin with a fabric square or rectangle. Use a large acrylic ruler to square up the left edge of the fabric. Make the first cut at a 45° angle to the left edge (see Bias Strip Diagram). Handle the diagonal edges carefully to avoid distorting the bias. To cut a strip, measure the desired width parallel to the 45° cut edge; cut. Continue cutting enough strips to total the length needed.

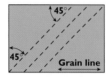

Bias Strip Diagram

ROTARY CUTTING

Instructions list pieces in the order in which they should be cut to make the best use of your fabrics. Always consider the fabric grain before cutting. The arrow on a pattern piece or template indicates which direction the fabric grain should run. One or more straight sides of the pattern piece or template should follow the fabric's lengthwise or crosswise grain.

The lengthwise grain, parallel to the selvage (the tightly finished edge), has the least amount of stretch. (Do not use the selvage of a woven fabric in a quilt. When washed, it may shrink more than the rest of the fabric.) Crosswise grain, perpendicular to the selvage, has a little

more give. The edge of any pattern piece that will be on the outside of a block or quilt should always be cut on the lengthwise grain. Be sure to press the fabric before cutting to remove any wrinkles or folds.

Using a Rotary Cutter

When cutting, keep an even pressure on the rotary cutter and make sure the blade is touching the edge of the ruler. The less you move your fabric when cutting, the more accurate you'll be.

CUTTING WITH TEMPLATES

About Scissors

Sharp scissor blades are vital to accurate cutting, but keeping them sharp is difficult because each use dulls the metal slightly. Cutting paper and plastic speeds the dulling process, so invest in a second pair for those materials and reserve your best scissors for fabric.

Make the Templates

For some quilts, you'll need to cut out the same shape multiple times. For accurate piecing later, the individual pieces should be identical to one another.

A template is a pattern made from extra-sturdy material so you can trace around it many times without wearing away the edges. You can make your own templates by duplicating printed patterns on plastic.

To make permanent templates, we recommend using easy-to-cut template plastic. This material lasts indefinitely, and its transparency allows you to trace the pattern directly onto its surface.

To make a template, lay the plastic over a printed pattern. Trace the pattern onto the plastic using a ruler and a permanent marker. This will ensure straight lines, accurate corners, and permanency. *Note:* If the pattern you are tracing is a half-pattern to begin with, you must first make a full-size pattern. To do so, fold a piece of tracing paper in half and crease; unfold. Lay the tracing paper over the half-pattern, aligning the crease with the fold line indicated on the pattern. Trace the half pattern. Then rotate the tracing paper, aligning the half pattern on the opposite side of the crease to trace the other half of the pattern. Use this full-size pattern to create your template.

For hand piecing and appliqué, make templates the exact size of the finished pieces, without seam allowances, by tracing the patterns' dashed lines. For machine piecing, make templates with the seam allowances included.

For easy reference, mark each template with its letter designation, grain line if noted, and block name. Verify the template's size by placing it over the printed pattern. Templates must be accurate or the error, however small, will compound many times as you assemble the quilt. To check the accuracy of your templates, make a test block before cutting the fabric pieces for an entire quilt.

Trace the Templates

To mark on fabric, use a special quilt marker that makes a thin, accurate line. Do not use a ballpoint or ink pen that may bleed if washed. Test all marking tools on a fabric scrap before using them.

To trace pieces that will be used for hand piecing or appliqué, place templates facedown on the wrong side of the fabric and trace; position the tracings at least ½" apart (see Diagram 1, Template A). The lines drawn on the fabric are the sewing lines. Mark cutting lines, or estimate by eye a seam allowance around each piece as you cut out the pieces. For hand piecing, add a ¼" seam allowance when cutting out the pieces; for hand appliqué, add a ³⁄₁₆" seam allowance.

Diagram 1

Templates used to make pieces for machine piecing have seam allowances included so you can use common lines for efficient cutting. Place templates facedown on the wrong side of the fabric and trace; position them without space in between (see Diagram 2, Template B). Using sharp scissors or a rotary cutter

and ruler, cut precisely on the drawn (cutting) lines.

Diagram 2

Templates for Angled Pieces

When two patchwork pieces come together and form an angled opening, a third piece must be set into this angle. This happens frequently when using diamond shapes.

For a design that requires setting in, a pinhole or window template makes it easy to mark the fabric with each shape's exact sewing and cutting lines and the exact point of each corner on the sewing line. By matching the corners of adjacent pieces, you'll be able to sew them together easily and accurately.

To make a pinhole template, lay template plastic over a pattern piece. Trace both the cutting and sewing lines onto the plastic. Carefully cut out the template on the cutting line. Using a sewing-machine needle or any large needle, make a hole in the template at each corner on the sewing line (matching points). The holes must be large enough for a pencil point or other fabric marker to poke through.

Trace Angled Pieces

To mark fabric using a pinhole template, lay it facedown on the wrong side of the fabric and trace. Using a pencil, mark dots on the fabric through the holes in the template to create matching points. Cut out the fabric piece on the drawn line, making sure the matching points are marked.

To mark fabric using a window template, lay it facedown on the wrong side of the fabric (see Diagram 3 on *page 94*). With a marking tool, mark the cutting line, sewing line, and each corner on the sewing line (matching points). Cut out the fabric piece on the cutting lines, making sure all pieces have sewing lines and matching points marked.

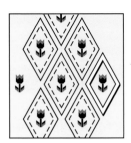

Diagram 3

APPLIQUÉ

Start Simple

We encourage beginners to select an appliqué design with straight lines and gentle curves. Learning to make sharp points and tiny stitches takes practice.

In the following instructions, we've used a stemmed flower motif as the appliqué example.

Baste the Seam Allowances

Begin by turning under the appliqué piece ³⁄₁₆" seam allowances; press. Some quilters like to thread-baste the folded edges to ensure proper placement. Edges that will be covered by other pieces don't need to be turned under.

For sharp points on tips, trim the seam allowance to within ⅛" of the stitching line; taper the sides gradually to ³⁄₁₆". Fold under the seam allowance remaining on the tips. Then turn the seam allowances under on both sides of the tips. The side seam allowances will overlap slightly at the tips, forming sharp points. Baste the folded edges in place. The turned seam allowances may form little pleats on the back side that you also

should baste in place. You'll remove the basting stitches after the shape has been appliquéd to the foundation.

Make Bias Stems

In order to curve gracefully, appliqué stems are cut on the bias. The strips for stems can be prepared in two ways. You can fold and press the strip in thirds. Or you can fold the bias strip in half lengthwise with the wrong side inside; press. Stitch ¼" in from the raw edges to keep them aligned. Fold the strip in half again, hiding the raw edges behind the first folded edge; press.

Position and Stitch

Pin the prepared appliqué pieces in place on the foundation using the position markings or referring to the block assembly diagram. If your pattern suggests it, mark the position for each piece on the foundation block before you begin. Overlap the flowers and stems as indicated.

Using thread in colors that match the fabrics, sew each stem and blossom onto the foundation with small slip stitches.

Catch only a few threads of the stem or flower fold with each stitch. Pull the stitches taut but not so tight that they pucker the fabric. You can use the needle's point to manipulate the appliqué edges as needed. Take an extra slip stitch at the point of a petal to secure it to the foundation.

You can use hand-quilting needles for appliqué stitching, but some quilters prefer a longer milliner's or straw needle. The extra needle length aids in tucking fabric under before taking slip stitches.

If the foundation fabric shows through the appliqué fabrics, cut away the foundation fabric. Trimming the foundation fabric also reduces the bulk of multiple layers when quilting. Carefully trim the underlying fabric to within ¼" of the appliqué stitches. Do not cut the appliqué fabric.

Fusible Appliqué

For quick-finish appliqué, use paper-backed fusible web. Then you can iron the shapes onto the foundation and add decorative stitching to the edges. This product consists of two layers, a fusible webbing lightly bonded to paper that peels off. The webbing adds a slight stiffness to the back of the appliqué pieces.

When you purchase this product, read the directions on the bolt end or packaging to make sure you're buying the right kind for your project. Some brands are specifically engineered to bond fabrics with no sewing at all. If you try to stitch fabric after it has bonded with one of these products, you may encounter difficulty. Some paper-backed fusible products are made exclusively for sewn edges; others work with or without stitching.

If you buy paper-backed fusible web from a bolt, be sure fusing instructions are included because the iron temperature and timing varies by brand. This information is usually on the paper backing.

With any of these products, the general procedure is to trace the pattern wrong side up onto the paper side of the fusible web. Then place the fusible web on the wrong side of the appliqué fabrics, paper side up, and use an iron to fuse the layers together. Then cut out the shapes, peel off the paper, turn the fabrics right side up, and fuse the shapes to the foundation fabric.

You also can fuse the fusible web and fabric together before tracing. You'll still need to trace templates wrong side up on the paper backing.

If you've used a no-sew fusible web, your appliqué is done. If not, finish the edges with hand or machine stitching.

FINISHING

Layering

Cut and piece the backing fabric to measure at least 3" bigger on all sides than the quilt top. Press all seam allowances open. With wrong sides together, layer the quilt top and backing fabric with the batting in between; baste. Quilt as desired.

Binding

The binding for most quilts is cut on the straight grain of the fabric. If your quilt has curved edges, cut the strips on the bias (opposite). The cutting instructions for projects in this book specify the number of binding strips or a total length needed to finish the quilt. The instructions also specify enough width for a French-fold or double-layer binding because it's easier to apply and adds durability.

Join the strips with diagonal seams to make one continuous binding strip (see Diagram 1). Trim the excess fabric, leaving ¼" seam allowances. Press the seam allowances open. Then, with the wrong sides together, fold under 1" at one end of the binding strip (see Diagram 2); press. Fold the strip in half lengthwise (see Diagram 3); press.

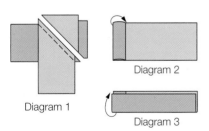

Diagram 1

Diagram 2

Diagram 3

Beginning in the center of one side, place the binding strip against the right side of the quilt top, aligning the binding strip's raw edges with the quilt top's raw edge (see Diagram 4). Beginning 1½" from the folded edge, sew through all layers, stopping ¼" from the corner. Backstitch, then clip the threads. Remove the quilt from under the sewing-machine presser foot.

Fold the binding strip upward (see Diagram 5), creating a diagonal fold, and finger-press.

Holding the diagonal fold in place with your finger, bring the binding strip down in line with the next edge, making a horizontal fold that aligns with the top edge of the quilt (see Diagram 6).

Start sewing again at the top of the horizontal fold, stitching through all layers. Sew around the quilt, turning each corner in the same manner.

When you return to the starting point, lap the binding strip inside the beginning fold (see Diagram 7). Finish sewing to the starting point (see Diagram 8). Trim the batting and backing fabric even with the quilt top edges.

Turn the binding over the edge of the quilt to the back. Hand-stitch the binding to the backing fabric, making sure to cover any machine stitching.

To make mitered corners on the back, hand-stitch the binding up to a corner; fold a miter in the binding. Take a stitch or two in the fold to secure it. Then stitch the binding in place up to the next corner. Finish each corner in the same manner.

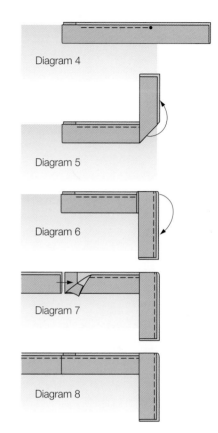

Diagram 4

Diagram 5

Diagram 6

Diagram 7

Diagram 8